To Dad
Happy Fathers Day 1987

Love Always
Denise & Roger. X

The GREAT BRITISH SONGBOOK

PAVILION
MICHAEL JOSEPH

THE GREAT BRITISH SONGBOOK

COMPILED BY
KINGSLEY AMIS
&
JAMES COCHRANE

First published in Great Britain in 1986 by
Pavilion Books Limited
196 Shaftesbury Avenue, London WC2H 8JL
in association with Michael Joseph Limited
27 Wrights Lane, Kensington, London W8 5TZ

Introduction, notes and selection © Kingsley Amis and James Cochrane

Design by Craig Dodd

British Library Cataloguing in Publication Data

The Great British songbook.
  1. Songs, English—Texts
  I. Amis, Kingsley   II. Cochrane, James
  784.3'05   PR1187

ISBN 1–85145–093–9

Typeset, printed and bound in Great Britain by
Butler and Tanner Limited, Frome and London

CONTENTS

Life and Laughter

INTRODUCTION

The popularity of songs and of singing them in company remains strong in this country, even in the age of piped music and the rock video. One of us was much struck recently by the enthusiastic response when, lateish on after a wedding, the party discovered they had available not only a piano and a pianist of sorts but a song-book full of the old favourites – 'If you were the only girl in the world', 'The rose of Tralee', 'Men of Harlech', 'Hello! hello! who's your lady friend?' and the rest. People joined in the singing because they knew the tunes in the first place, of course, or could pick them up, but it was no less important that for once they had the words in front of them and so could stay in the action instead of having to drop out at the end of the couple of lines they could recall. And every Christmastime there must be hundreds of occasions when an impromptu carol-singing which all would enjoy fades away or never starts because nobody could get further than the first verse of 'While shepherds watched'. There may even be those who would like to be able to have a shot at singing 'Jerusalem' or 'Sussex by the sea' solo, for the fun of it.

So what we are doing in this book is providing the words everybody has forgotten for the tunes everybody remembers. Well, a great many people remember. We made it a strict rule that every song must be a *song*, that nothing should go into the selection unless at least one of us knew the tune. One editor tried to smuggle in 'Crossing the bar' (Tennyson) on the grounds that, although admittedly he had never heard it sung, such obvious lyric material *must* have been set to music at some time, but this was sternly vetoed by the other. We naturally excluded poems that have beyond all doubt been set, but to music not apt to be widely remembered, which means for example that those who feel like chanting Benjamin Britten's setting of poems by Donne over a convivial glass will have to look elsewhere for the words. Indeed it is remarkable, and rather sad, that those usually thought of as important or serious or classical composers should have written so few vocal pieces that have established themselves in lasting popular favour: in this collection only 'Where'er you walk' (Handel), 'Song to Silvia'/'Who is Sylvia?' (Schubert), 'Hark, the herald angels sing' (Mendelssohn) and perhaps a couple more.

Since we are naturally hoping to attract not just would-be singers but general readers too, we made it another broad rule to include nothing not worth reading for itself, interesting enough at least to stand up without its tune. This turned out to restrict our choice very little, though in a few late cases, particularly of songs from the First and Second World Wars, we slipped the odd one in less for any literary merit than because it seemed to us to be a faithful and vivid expression of its period.

Many of the pieces in this book had an earlier and separate life as poems before attracting the attention of a composer, sometimes many years afterwards. 'To be a pilgrim' is a very clear instance, the work of a parson-poet so puritanical that he forbade all singing in his church as a distraction from the true act of worship. (To be consistent he should have banned any sort of poetry too, like psalms.) Most hymns came along in this way but not most carols, whose tunes often preceded the words now sung to them. Thus the tale of Good King Wenceslas is not a legend of old Bohemia but the invention of another parson-poet, early Victorian this time, who wrote the words to fit the sixteenth–century tune.

Other songs had music or a musician involved in their very conception. Now and again, from 'Tom Bowling' to 'Mad dogs and Englishmen', writer, composer and performer were one and the same. More often what we might now call a team would have worked together from the start, or at least the writer had all along intended his words for setting to music, very likely by a particular composer. This must have been the rule with Shakespeare's songs. He outshone other dramatists in plenty of ways, but nowhere more strikingly than in this department. Even the slightest of his songs are self-sufficient poems, something his contemporaries (and successors) never achieved.

At whatever stage the composer might have come into the story, and whether the finished product was to be sung in church or music-hall, by many voices or one, the words retained their importance and autonomy. In vocal music on a different level, in operas, choral works, even recital-room songs in the German tradition, the words are secondary, and the performance can be enjoyed to quite a large degree by people with no understanding of the language. Significantly, operatic singers of international reputation regularly get away with being verbally unintelligible in English and in English-speaking countries. (Perhaps not in Italian and in Italy.) They would not have been so lucky on a variety stage or in an old-style garrison theatre.

In consequence the lyrics of popular songs had to be worked on, given careful finish: shoddy rhyming, awkward phraseology, would have been too patently exposed. Some originality or freshness of expression, even some wit, were called for. No obscurity was to be suffered gladly, and if some words and references are puzzling today, the chances are they were clear enough to their original audiences. The other main requirement was that the subject, the message, the characters or events described or commemorated must be fully recognisable and acceptable, conveying a mood and an outlook all could share. This is not a recipe for good poetry, any more than anything else is, but its products even now retain something of the immediacy and glow they had in the days when they were still fully current and habitually sung.

The golden age of British song, as of much else, roughly coincides with the Victorian period, plus a few years' extension to 1914. Other guillotines descended in 1945 and whichever year in the 1960s marked the final demise of the song as a thing of the present. Up till the earliest of these dates song-lyrics, especially those intended for performance on stage, continued to be conscientiously crafted, but the rise of the gramophone record, wireless broad-casting and the sound-film, with the attendant multiplication of quantity, seems to have brought into being a multitude of hacks who simply threw clichés together: Tin-Pan Alley (first US mention 1908, UK 1934) was in business. But one cannot help noticing that the last acknowledged British poets to produce words that could be turned into memorable songs were Housman, Newbolt, Kipling and Masefield, of whom the youngest (Masefield) was born in 1878. These things run deep.

Taken together, the popular songs we have collected draw some sort of composite portrait of the British character as seen in a particular social period. They seem to reflect a people much given to sentimentality, especially about sex and home, but at the same time wary of emotional excess; respectful of institutions but prepared to poke fun at them; not inclined to sneer at ordinary life or humble aspirations, in fact ready to salute merit there; devoted to harmless amusements and fond of frivolity and drink; deeply patriotic without much jingoism or undue sense of superiority. More is said on this subject in the preface to the section on War and Patriotism; for the moment we suggest merely that it is very British of the British to have warmed to a parody of one of their most cherished nationalistic songs ('mar-ri-ed to a mer-mi-ade'), and that for a supposedly insular people they have shown themselves quick enough to adopt the songs of other nations.

These latter have of course come chiefly from Ireland and America. Mindful of our commitment to a 'British' selection, we restricted ourselves to those which, without their origins being lost sight of, are in our estimation about as likely to be sung at a British gathering as any native product.

Within our four categories we have arranged songs roughly in the chronological order of their composition, as far as this can be determined, which with so many anonymous pieces present is sometimes not very far.

When what a poet or lyric-writer wrote differs from what is habitually sung, we have generally preferred the latter. So for instance we print 'To be a pilgrim' not in Bunyan's original version of 1678 but as revised, with a completely different opening, by an unknown hand in the *English Hymnal* of 1906. And Britons never 'shall' be slaves here, not 'will' as James Thomson, a Scot following Scottish usage, naturally had them.

Finally: a good tune has often excused or disguised inadequate words, but it can also distract some attention from ones that are interesting or better and appear to their advantage on the page. In our search for material we encountered many pleasant surprises of this sort, from 'Johnny, I hardly knew ye' to 'Polly Perkins of Paddington Green'. Now is the moment to say that the choice of pieces is entirely ours and that, apart from the limitation of length, we have been guided by our own taste and nothing else. The result shows at any rate the immense range of British popular song as it was, and parts of it might come as a revelation to some of those young (or youngish) unfortunates who are unaware of any other vocal music than the sort aimed specifically at them.

KA & JC, 1986

WAR & PATRIOTISM

Land of Hope and Glory

God Save the Queen

Rule Britannia

Whole books have been written trying to ascertain the author and the composer of the National Anthem, but establishing only that neither can have been a single individual. The words and tune in something like their present form seem to have been first brought together in the mid-eighteenth century at about the time of Bonnie Prince Charlie's invasion of England. Attempts to have the pugnacious and effective second verse toned down have been persistent but unavailing, though there can be very few people alive who have ever heard it sung.*

It is difficult and perhaps tasteless to take any objective view of a tune so rich in association, but that of 'God save the Queen' cannot be said to come triumphantly well out of a comparison with either 'Land of my fathers' or 'The star-spangled banner'. Unlike them, however, it can be sung without effort by anybody not actually tone-deaf and it allows of being cut off without violence after six bars.

We might have considered saying that the British, as shown in their national songs, were without 'any' rather than 'much' jingoism if it had not been for 'Land of hope and glory', much too popular to leave out but embarrassing to some in its sentiments ('mightier yet'?). Nor is Elgar's tune irreproachable. An (English) organist once said he could just about stand it up to the three descending notes in the accompaniment before the repetition of 'God, who made thee mighty', at which he would collapse in disgust.

But if British patriotism has on occasion overreached itself, it has perhaps softened the offence by being tolerant internally, as of Scottish and Welsh patriotism by the English. Collectively, the British have also been hospitable to songs in that kind of vein from Ireland and the USA. Some of these have been naturalised here for a long time, and the senior of us remembers joining in with 'Marching through Georgia' fifty years ago, without knowing who was marching or why.

'Recessional' has been taken in the past as a piece of 'jingoism' and imperialist swagger by that well-known fascist, Kipling. Reading its text shows it to be a solemn warning against the abuse of British power. The despised and dangerous 'lesser breeds without the Law' are not Indians or Africans but European nationalists, chiefly German – rather to the point in the years before 1914. (The poem was written specifically to commemorate Queen Victoria's diamond jubilee in 1897, an occasion cut out for tub-thumping. It is interesting to compare it with A.E. Housman's poem '1887' on the golden jubilee.)

The songs British servicemen might collectively sing in wartime, as opposed to ones heard in performance, were apt to be distinctly unwarlike, indeed to convey a strong desire to be a long way off, preferably in contact with booze and women. Others, their words run up on the spot to popular tunes of the day, and often of only local interest, were directed not towards the war as such but against blundering politicians ('The D-Day dodgers', Italy 1944) or arrogant base-wallahs ('Don't freeze us in', Belgium 1945). In a different spirit, 'Johnny, I Hardly Knew Ye' provides a powerful comment on any temptation to glorify war.

*Diplomatic considerations might have led to its omission at the coronation of H.M. Queen Elizabeth II in 1953.

14

Rule Britannia

When Britain first, at Heaven's command,
    Arose from out the azure main, (*twice*)
This was the charter of the land,
    And guardian angels sang this strain –
      'Rule, Britannia! Britannia rule the waves;
      Britons never, never, never shall be slaves.'

The nations, not so blest as thee,
    Must in their turns to tyrants fall; (*twice*)
While thou shalt flourish great and free,
    The dread and envy of them all.
      Rule, Britannia! etc.

Still more majestic shalt thou rise,
    More dreadful from each foreign stroke; (*twice*)
As the loud blast that tears the skies
    Serves but to root thy native oak.
      Rule, Britannia! etc.

Thee haughty tyrants ne'er shall tame;
    All their attempts to bend thee down (*twice*)
Will but arouse thy generous flame,
    And work their woe and thy renown.
      Rule, Britannia! etc.

To thee belongs the rural reign;
    Thy cities shall with commerce shine; (*twice*)
All thine shall be the subject main,
    And every shore it circles thine.
      Rule, Britannia! etc.

The Muses, still with freedom found,
    Shall to thy happy coast repair: (*twice*)
Blest isle with matchless beauty crowned,
    And manly hearts to guard the fair.
      Rule, Britannia! etc.

James Thomson 1700–1748

God Save the Queen

God save our gracious Queen,
Long live our noble Queen,
   God save the Queen!
Send her victorious,
Happy and glorious,
Long to reign over us;
   God save the Queen!

O Lord our God, arise,
Scatter her enemies
   And make them fall;
Confound their politics,
Frustrate their knavish tricks,
On Thee our hopes we fix,
   Oh, save us all!

Thy choicest gifts in store
On her be pleased to pour;
   Long may she reign;
May she defend our laws,
And ever give us cause
To sing with heart and voice,
   God save the Queen!

Anon.

Heart of Oak

Come, cheer up, my lads! 'tis to glory we steer,
To add something more to this wonderful year;
To honour we call you, not press you like slaves –
For who are so free as we sons of the waves?
      Heart of oak are our ships,
      Heart of oak are our men;
      We always are ready;
      Steady, boys, steady;
We'll fight and we'll conquer again and again.

We ne'er see our foes but we wish 'em to stay,
They never see us but they wish us away;
If they run, why, we follow, and run 'em ashore,
For if they won't fight us, we cannot do more.
      Heart of oak, etc.

They swear they'll invade us, these terrible foes,
They frighten our women, our children and beaux;
But should their flat-bottoms in darkness get o'er,
Still Britons they'll find to receive them on shore.
      Heart of oak, etc.

We'll still make 'em run, and we'll still make 'em sweat,
In spite of the devil and Brussels Gazette;
Then cheer up, my lads, with one heart let us sing,
Our soldiers, our sailors, our statesmen, and King.
      Heart of oak, etc.

David Garrick 1717–1779

The British Grenadiers

Some talk of Alexander, and some of Hercules;
Of Hector and Lysander, and such great names as these;
But of all the world's brave heroes, there's none that can compare
With a tow, row, row, row, row, row, row, for the British Grenadier.

Those heroes of antiquity ne'er saw a cannon ball,
Or knew the force of powder to slay their foes withal;
But our brave boys do know it, and banish all their fears,
Sing tow, row, row, row, row, row, row, for the British Grenadiers.

Whene'er we are commanded to storm the palisades,
Our leaders march with fusees, and we with hand grenades;
We throw them from the glacis about the enemies' ears,
Sing tow, row, row, row, row, row, row, for the British Grenadiers.

And when the siege is over, we to the town repair,
The townsmen cry, Hurrah, boys, here comes a Grenadier,
Here come the Grenadiers, my boys, who know no doubts or fears,
Sing tow, row, row, row, row, row, row, for the British Grenadiers,

Then let us fill a bumper, and drink a health to those
Who carry caps and pouches, and wear the loupèd clothes;
May they and their commanders live happy all their years,
With a tow, row, row, row, row, row, row, for the British Grenadiers.

Anon.

18

For a' That

Is there, for honest poverty,
    That hings his head, an' a' that?
The coward slave, we pass him by,
    We dare be poor for a' that!
      For a' that, an' a' that,
        Our toils obscure, an' a' that;
      The rank is but the guinea's stamp;
        The man's the gowd for a' that.

What though on hamely fare we dine,
    Wear hodden-gray, an' a' that;
Gie fools their silks, and knaves their wine,
    A man's a man for a' that.
      For a' that, an' a' that,
        Their tinsel show, an' a' that;
      The honest man, tho' e'er sae poor,
        Is king o' men for a' that.

Ye see yon birkie, ca'd a lord,
    Wha struts, an' stares, an' a' that;
Tho' hundreds worship at his word,
    He's but a cuif for a' that:
      For a' that, an' a' that,
        His riband, star, an' a' that,
      The man o' independent mind,
        He looks and laughs at a' that.

A prince can mak a belted knight,
    A marquis, duke, an' a' that;
But an honest man's aboon his might,
    Guid faith, he mauna fa that!
      For a' that, an' a' that,
        Their dignities, an' a' that,
      The pith o' sense, an' pride o' worth,
        Are higher rank than a' that.

Then let us pray that come it may
    (As come it will for a' that)
That Sense and Worth o'er a' the earth,
    Shall bear the gree an' a' that!
      For a' that, an' a' that,
        It's coming yet, for a' that,
      That man to man the world o'er
        Shall brithers be for a' that.

Scots Wha Hae

Scots, wha hae wi' Wallace bled,
Scots, wham Bruce has aften led,
Welcome to your gory bed,
    Or to victory!

Now's the day, and now's the hour;
See the front o' battle lour,
See approach proud Edward's power –
    Chains and slavery!

Wha will be a traitor knave?
Wha can fill a coward's grave?
Wha sae base as be a slave? –
    Let him turn, and flee!

Wha for Scotland's King and Law
Freedom's sword will strongly draw,
Freeman stand or freeman fa',
    Let him follow me!

By Oppression's woes and pains,
By your sons in servile chains,
We will drain our dearest veins,
    But they shall be free!

Lay the proud usurpers low!
Tyrants fall in every foe!
Liberty's in every blow!
    Let us do, or die!

Robert Burns 1759–1796

19

Ye Mariners of England

Ye Mariners of England
　That guard our native seas!
Whose flag has braved a thousand years
　The battle and the breeze!
Your glorious standard launch again
　To match another foe;
And sweep through the deep,
　While the stormy winds do blow!
While the battle rages loud and long
　And the stormy winds do blow.

The spirits of your fathers
　Shall start from every wave –
For the deck it was their field of fame,
　And Ocean was their grave:
Where Blake and mighty Nelson fell
　Your manly hearts shall glow,
As ye sweep through the deep,
　While the stormy winds do blow!
While the battle rages loud and long
　And the stormy winds do blow.

Britannia needs no bulwarks,
　No towers along the steep;
Her march is o'er the mountain-waves,
　Her home is on the deep.
With thunders from her native oak
　She quells the floods below,
As they roar on the shore,
　When the stormy winds do blow!
When the battle rages loud and long,
　And the stormy winds do blow.

The meteor flag of England
　Shall yet terrific burn;
Till danger's troubled night depart
　And the star of peace return.
Then, then, ye ocean-warriors!
　Our song and feast shall flow
To the fame of your name,
　When the storm has ceased to blow!
When the fiery fight is heard no more,
　And the storm has ceased to blow.

Thomas Campbell 1777–1844

The Minstrel Boy

The Minstrel Boy to the war is gone,
    In the ranks of death you'll find him;
His father's sword he has girded on,
    And his wild harp slung behind him.
'Land of song!' said the warrior-bard,
    'Though all the world betrays thee,
One sword, at least, thy rights shall guard,
    One faithful harp shall praise thee.'

The Minstrel fell! – but the foeman's chain
    Could not bring his proud soul under;
The harp he loved ne'er spoke again,
    For he tore its chords asunder;
And said, 'No chains shall sully thee,
    Thou soul of love and bravery!
Thy songs wcrc madc for the pure and free,
    They shall never sound in slavery.'

Thomas Moore 1779–1852

The Harp that once through Tara's Halls

The harp that once through Tara's halls,
    The soul of music shed,
Now hangs as mute on Tara's walls
    As if that soul were fled.
So sleeps the pride of former days,
    So glory's thrill is o'er,
And hearts, that once beat high for praise,
    Now feel that pulse no more!

No more to chiefs and ladies bright
    The harp of Tara swells:
The chord, alone, that breaks at night,
    Its tale of ruin tells.
Thus Freedom now so seldom wakes,
    The only throb she gives,
Is when some heart indignant breaks,
    To shew that still she lives!

Thomas Moore 1779–1852

The Song of the Western Men

A good sword and a trusty hand!
  A merry heart and true!
King James's men shall understand
  What Cornish lads can do.

And have they fixed the where and when?
  And shall Trelawny die?
Here's twenty thousand Cornish men
  Will know the reason why!

Out spake their captain brave and bold,
  A merry wight was he:
'If London Tower were Michael's hold,
  We'd set Trelawny free!

'We'll cross the Tamar, land to land,
  The Severn is no stay,
With "one and all" and hand in hand,
  And who shall bid us nay?

'And when we come to London Wall,
  A pleasant sight to view,
Come forth! come forth! ye cowards all,
  Here's men as good as you.

'Trelawny he's in keep and hold,
  Trelawny he may die;
But here's twenty thousand Cornish bold
  Will know the reason why!'

Robert S. Hawker 1803–1875

The Wearing of the Green

Oh, Paddy dear, and did you hear the news that's going round?
The shamrock is forbid by law to grow on Irish ground;
Saint Patrick's Day no more we'll keep, his colours can't be seen,
For there's a cruel law against the wearing of the green.
I met with Napper Tandy, and he took me by the hand,
And he said, 'How's poor old Ireland, and how does she stand?'
She's the most distressful country that ever yet was seen;
They're hanging men and women there for wearing of the green.

Then since the colour we must wear is England's cruel red,
Sure Ireland's sons will ne'er forget the blood that they have shed;
You may take the shamrock from your hat, and cast it on the sod,
But 'twill take root and flourish there, tho' underfoot 'tis trod.
When law can stop the blades of grass from growing as they grow,
And when the leaves in summer-time their verdure dare not show,
Then I will change the colour that I wear in my caubeen;
But till that day, please God, I'll stick to wearing of the green.

But if at last our colour should be torn from Ireland's heart,
Her sons, with shame and sorrow, from the dear old isle will part;
I've heard whisper of a country that lies beyond the sea,
Where rich and poor stand equal in the light of freedom's day.
Oh, Erin! must we leave you, driven by a tyrant's hand?
Must we ask a mother's blessing from a strange and distant land?
Where the cruel cross of England shall never more be seen,
And where, please God, we'll live and die still wearing of the green.

Dion Boucicault c. 1820–1890

Men of Harlech

Hark! I hear the foe advancing,
Barbèd steeds are proudly prancing;
Helmets, in the sunbeams glancing,
   Glitter through the trees.
Men of Harlech, lie ye dreaming?
See ye not their falchions gleaming,
While their pennons gaily streaming
   Flutter in the breeze?
From the rocks rebounding,
Let the war-cry sounding
   Summon all
   At Cambria's call,
The haughty foe surrounding.
Men of Harlech, on to glory!
See, your banner fam'd in story
Waves these burning words before ye,
   'Britain scorns to yield!'

'Mid the fray, see dead and dying,
Friend and foe together lying;
All around the arrows flying
   Scatter sudden death!
Frightened steeds are wildly neighing,
Brazen trumpets hoarsely braying,
Wounded men for mercy praying
   With their parting breath!
See – they're in disorder! –
Comrades, keep close order!
   Ever they
   Shall rue the day
They ventured o'er the border!
Now the Saxon flees before us;
Victory's banner floateth o'er us!
Raise the loud, exulting chorus,
   'Britain wins the field!'

Thomas Oliphant 1799–1873

24

The Star-Spangled Banner

O say, can you see, by the dawn's early light,
    What so proudly we hailed at the twilight's last gleaming –
Whose broad stripes and bright stars, through the clouds of the fight,
    O'er the ramparts we watched were so gallantly streaming!
And the rocket's red glare, the bombs bursting in air,
Gave proof through the night that our flag was still there;
O say, does that star-spangled banner yet wave
O'er the land of the free, and the home of the brave?

On that shore dimly seen through the mists of the deep,
    Where the foe's haughty host in dread silence reposes,
What is that which the breeze, o'er the towering steep,
    As it fitfully blows, now conceals, now discloses?
Now it catches the gleam of the morning's first beam,
In full glory reflected now shines on the stream;
'Tis the star-spangled banner; Oh long may it wave
O'er the land of the free, and the home of the brave!

And where is that band who so vauntingly swore
    That the havoc of war and the battle's confusion
A home and a country should leave us no more?
    Their blood has washed out their foul footsteps' pollution.
No refuge could save the hireling and slave
From the terror of flight, or the gloom of the grave;
And the star-spangled banner in triumph doth wave
O'er the land of the free, and the home of the brave.

O! thus be it ever, when freemen shall stand
    Between their loved homes and the war's desolation!
Blest with victory and peace, may the heav'n-rescued land
    Praise the power that hath made and preserved us a nation.
Then conquer we must, when our cause it is just,
And this be our motto – 'In God is our trust':
And the star-spangled banner in triumph shall wave
O'er the land of the free, and the home of the brave.

Francis Scott Key 1779–1843

25

When Johnny Comes Marching Home

When Johnny comes marching home again,
    Hurrah! Hurrah!
We'll give him a hearty welcome then;
    Hurrah! Hurrah!
The men will cheer, the boys will shout,
The ladies they will all turn out;
    And we'll all feel gay
    When Johnny comes marching home.

The old church bells will peal with joy,
    Hurrah! Hurrah!
To welcome home our darling boy;
    Hurrah! Hurrah!
The village lads and lasses say
With roses they will strew the way;
    And we'll all, etc.

Get ready for the jubilee,
    Hurrah! Hurrah!
We'll give the hero three times three;
    Hurrah! Hurrah!
The laurel wreath is ready now,
To place upon his royal brow;
    And we'll all, etc.

Let love and friendship on that day,
    Hurrah! Hurrah!
Their choicest treasures then display,
    Hurrah! Hurrah!
And let each one perform some part
To fill with joy the warrior's heart;
    And we'll all, etc.

Anon.

26

Johnny, I Hardly Knew Ye

While going the road to sweet Athy,
    Hurroo! Hurroo!
While going the road to sweet Athy,
    Hurroo! Hurroo!
While going the road to sweet Athy,
A stick in my hand and a drop in my eye,
A doleful damsel I heard cry:
    Och, Johnny, I hardly knew ye!
      With drums and guns and guns and drums,
        The enemy nearly slew ye!
        My darling, dear, you look so queer,
    Och, Johnny, I hardly knew ye!

Where are your eyes that looked so mild?
    Hurroo! Hurroo!
Where are your eyes that looked so mild?
    Hurroo! Hurroo!
Where are your eyes that looked so mild
When my poor heart you first beguiled?
Why did you run from me and the child?
    Och, Johnny, I hardly knew ye!
      With drums and guns, etc.

Where are the legs with which you run?
    Hurroo! Hurroo!
Where are the legs with which you run?
    Hurroo! Hurroo!
Where are the legs with which you run,
When you went to carry a gun? –
Indeed your dancing days are done!
    Och, Johnny, I hardly knew ye!
      With drums and guns, etc.

It grieved my heart to see you sail,
    Hurroo! Hurroo!
It grieved my heart to see you sail,
    Hurroo! Hurroo!
It grieved my heart to see you sail,
Though from my heart you took leg bail, –
Like a cod you're doubled up head and tail,
    Och, Johnny, I hardly knew ye!
      With drums and guns, etc.

'You haven't an arm and you haven't a leg,
    Hurroo! Hurroo!
You haven't an arm and you haven't a leg,
    Hurroo! Hurroo!
You haven't an arm and you haven't a leg,
You're an eyeless, noseless, chickenless egg:
You'll have to be put in a bowl to beg,
    Och, Johnny, I hardly knew ye!
      With drums and guns, etc.

'I'm happy for to see you home,
    Hurroo! Hurroo!
I'm happy for to see you home,
    Hurroo! Hurroo!
I'm happy for to see you home,
All from the island of Sulloon.
So low in flesh, so high in bone,
    Och, Johnny, I hardly knew ye!
      With drums and guns, etc.

'But sad as it is to see you so,
    Hurroo! Hurroo!
But sad as it is to see you so,
    Hurroo! Hurroo!
But sad as it is to see you so,
And to think of you now as an object of woe,
Your Peggy'll still keep ye on as her beau.
    Och, Johnny, I hardly knew ye!
      With drums and guns, etc.

Anon.

Battle Hymn of the Republic

Mine eyes have seen the glory of the coming of the Lord;
He is trampling out the vintage where the grapes of wrath are stored;
He hath loosed the fatal lightning of his terrible swift sword:
   His Truth is marching on.

I have seen him in the watch-fires of a hundred circling camps;
They have builded him an altar in the evening dews and damps;
I have read his righteous sentence by the dim and flaring lamps:
   His Day is marching on.

I have read a fiery gospel, writ in burnished rows of steel:
'As you deal with my contemners, so with you my grace shall deal;'
Let the Hero born of woman crush the serpent with his heel,
   Since God is marching on.

He has sounded forth the trumpet that shall never call retreat;
He is sifting out the hearts of men before his judgement-seat;
O be swift, my soul, to answer him; be jubilant, my feet!
   Our God is marching on.

In the beauty of the lilies Christ was born across the sea,
With a glory in his bosom that transfigures you and me;
As he died to make men holy, let us die to make men free,
   While God is marching on.

He is coming like the glory of the morning on the wave;
He is wisdom to the mighty, he is succour to the brave;
So the world shall be his footstool, and the soul of time his slave:
   Our God is marching on.

Julia Ward Howe 1819–1910

Marching through Georgia

Bring the good old bugle, boys, we'll sing another song,
Sing it with a spirit that will start the world along,
Sing it as we used to sing it, fifty thousand strong,
   While we were marching through Georgia.
      Hurrah! hurrah! we bring the jubilee!
      Hurrah! hurrah! the flag that makes you free!
      So we sang the chorus from Atlanta to the sea,
      While we were marching through Georgia.

How the darkies shouted when they heard the joyful sound;
How the turkeys gobbled which our commissary found;
How the sweet potatoes even started from the ground,
   While we were marching through Georgia.
      Hurrah! hurrah! etc.

Yes, and there were Union men who wept with joyful tears,
When they saw the honoured flag they had not seen for years,
Hardly could they be restrained from breaking forth in cheers,
   While we were marching through Georgia.
      Hurrah! hurrah! etc.

'Sherman's dashing Yankee boys will never reach the coast,'
So the saucy rebels said, and 'twas a handsome boast;
Had they not forgot, alas, to reckon with the host,
   While we were marching through Georgia.
      Hurrah! hurrah! etc.

So we made a thoroughfare for Freedom and her train,
Sixty miles in latitude, three hundred to the main;
Treason fled before us, for resistance was in vain,
   While we were marching through Georgia.
      Hurrah! hurrah! etc.

H.C. Work 1832–1884

Land of Hope and Glory

Dear Land of Hope, thy hope is crowned.
   God make thee mightier yet!
On Sov'ran brows, beloved, renowned,
   Once more thy crown is set.
Thine equal laws, by Freedom gained,
   Have ruled thee well and long;
By Freedom gained, by Truth maintained,
   Thine Empire shall be strong.

Land of Hope and Glory, Mother of the Free,
How shall we extol thee, who are born of thee?
Wider still and wider shall thy bounds be set;
God, who made thee mighty, make thee mightier yet.

Thy fame is ancient as the days,
   As Ocean large and wide;
A pride that dares, and heeds not praise,
   A stern and silent pride:
Not that false joy that dreams content
   With what our sires have won;
The blood a hero sire hath spent
   Still nerves a hero son.
      Land of Hope and Glory, etc.

A.C. Benson 1862–1925

Recessional

God of our fathers, known of old,
   Lord of our far-flung battle-line,
Beneath whose awful Hand we hold
   Dominion over palm and pine –
Lord God of Hosts, be with us yet,
Lest we forget – lest we forget!

The tumult and the shouting dies;
   The Captains and the Kings depart:
Still stands Thine ancient sacrifice,
   An humble and a contrite heart.
Lord God of Hosts, be with us yet,
Lest we forget – lest we forget!

Far-called, our navies melt away;
   On dune and headland sinks the fire:
Lo, all our pomp of yesterday
   Is one with Nineveh and Tyre!
Judge of the Nations, spare us yet,
Lest we forget – lest we forget!

If, drunk with sight of power, we loose
   Wild tongues that have not Thee in awe –
Such boasting as the Gentiles use
   Or lesser breeds without the Law –
Lord God of Hosts, be with us yet,
Lest we forget, lest we forget!

For heathen heart that puts her trust
   In reeking tube and iron shard –
All valiant dust that builds on dust,
   And guarding calls not Thee to guard –
For frantic boast and foolish word,
Thy mercy on Thy people, Lord!

Rudyard Kipling 1865–1936

Boots

We're foot – slog – slog – slog – sloggin' over Africa –
Foot – foot – foot – foot – sloggin' over Africa –
(Boots – boots – boots – boots – movin' up and down again!)
    There's no discharge in the war!

Seven – six – eleven – five – nine-an'-twenty mile to-day –
Four – eleven – seventeen – thirty-two the day before –
(Boots – boots – boots – boots – movin' up and down again!)
    There's no discharge in the war!

Don't – don't – don't – don't – look at what's in front of you.
(Boots – boots – boots – boots – movin' up an' down again);
Men – men – men – men – men go mad with watchin' 'em,
    An' there's no discharge in the war!

Try – try – try – try – to think o' something different –
Oh – my – God – keep – me from goin' lunatic!
(Boots – boots – boots – boots – movin' up an' down again!)
    There's no discharge in the war!

Count – count – count – count – the bullets in the bandoliers.
If – your – eyes – drop – they will get atop o' you!
(Boots – boots – boots – boots – movin' up and down again!) –
    There's no discharge in the war!

We – can – stick – out – 'unger, thirst, an' weariness,
But – not – not – not – not the chronic sight of 'em –
Boots – boots – boots – boots – movin' up an' down again,
    An' there's no discharge in the war!

'T'ain't – so – bad – by – day because o' company,
But night – brings – long – strings – o' forty thousand million
Boots – boots – boots – boots – movin' up an' down again.
    There's no discharge in the war!

I – 'ave – marched – six – weeks in 'Ell an' certify
It – is – not – fire – devils, dark or anything,
But boots – boots – boots – boots – movin' up an' down again,
    An' there's no discharge in the war!

Rudyard Kipling 1865–1936

32

The Yeomen of England

Who were the Yeomen, the Yeomen of England?
The freemen were the Yeomen, the freemen of England!
    Stout were the bows they bore
    When they went out to war,
Stouter their courage for the honour of England!
    And Spaniards and Dutchmen,
    And Frenchmen and such men,
      As foemen did curse them,
      The bowmen of England!
    No other land could nurse them
    But their motherland, Old England!
And on her broad bosom did they ever thrive!

Where are the Yeomen, the Yeomen of England?
In homestead and in cottage, they still dwell in England!
    Stained with the ruddy tan,
    God's air doth give a man,
Free as the winds that fan the broad breast of England!
    And Spaniards and Dutchmen,
    And Frenchmen and such men,
      As foemen may curse them,
      The Yeomen of England!
    No other land can nurse them,
    But their motherland, Old England!
And on her broad bosom shall they ever thrive!

Basil Hood

Drake's Drum

Drake he's in his hammock an' a thousand mile away,
    (Capten, art tha sleepin' there below?),
Slung atween the round shot in Nombre Dios Bay,
    An' dreamin' arl the time o' Plymouth Hoe.
Yarnder lumes the Island, yarnder lie the ships,
    Wi' sailor lads a-dancin' heel-an'-toe,
An' the shore-lights flashin', an' the night-tide dashin',
    He sees et arl so plainly as he saw et long ago.

Drake he was a Devon man, an' ruled the Devon seas,
    (Capten, art tha sleepin' there below?),
Rovin' tho' his death fell, he went wi' heart at ease,
    An' dreamin' arl the time o' Plymouth Hoe.
'Take my drum to England, hang et by the shore,
    Strike et when your powder's runnin' low;
If the Dons sight Devon, I'll quit the port o' Heaven,
    An' drum them up the Channel as we drummed them long ago.'

Drake he's in his hammock till the great Armadas come,
    (Capten, art tha sleepin' there below?),
Slung atween the round shot, listenin' for the drum,
    An' dreamin' arl the time o' Plymouth Hoe.
Call him on the deep sea, call him up the Sound,
    Call him when ye sail to meet the foe;
Where the old trade's plyin' an' the old flag flyin'
    They shall fnd him ware an' wakin', as they found him long ago!

Sir Henry Newbolt 1862–1938

Sussex by the Sea

Now is the time for marching,
Now let your hearts be gay,
Hark to the merry bugles,
Sounding along our way.
So let your voices ring, my boys,
And take the time from me,
And I'll sing you a song as we march along
Of Sussex by the sea!
  For we're the men from Sussex,
  Sussex by the sea.
  We plough and sow and reap and mow,
  And useful men are we;
  And when you go to Sussex,
  Whoever you may be,
  You may tell them all that we stand or fall
  For Sussex by the sea!
  Oh Sussex, Sussex by the sea!
  Good old Sussex by the sea!
  You may tell them all that we stand or fall
  For Sussex by the sea!

Up in the morning early,
Start at the break of day;
March till the evening shadows
Tell us it's time to stay.
We're always moving on, my boys,
So take the time from me,
And sing this song as we march along
Of Sussex by the sea!
  For we're the men, etc.

Sometimes your feet are weary,
Sometimes the way is long,
Sometimes the day is dreary,
Sometimes the world goes wrong;
But if you let your voices ring,
Your care will fly away,
So we'll sing a song as we march along,
Of Sussex by the sea!
  For we're the men, etc.

Light is the love of a soldier,
That's what the ladies say;
Lightly he goes a-wooing,
Lightly he rides away.
In love and war we always are
As fair as fair can be,
And a soldier boy is the ladies' joy
In Sussex by the sea!
  For we're the men, etc.

Far o'er the seas we wander,
Wide thro' the world we roam;
Far from the kind hearts yonder,
Far from the dear old home;
But ne'er shall we forget, my boys,
And true we'll ever be
To the girls so kind that we left behind
In Sussex by the sea!
  For we're the men, etc.

W. Ward-Higgs (d.1936)

35

Tipperary

Up to mighty London came an Irishman one day,
As the streets are paved with gold, sure ev'ry one was gay,
Singing songs of Piccadilly, Strand and Leicester Square,
Till Paddy got excited, then he shouted to them there:
    It's a long way to Tipperary,
    It's a long way to go;
    It's a long way to Tipperary,
    To the sweetest girl I know!
    Goodbye Piccadilly! Farewell, Leicester Square!
    It's a long, long way to Tipperary,
    But my heart's right there!

Paddy wrote a letter to his Irish Molly O',
Saying 'Should you not receive it, write and let me know!
If I make mistakes in spelling, Molly dear,' said he,
'Remember it's the pen that's bad, don't lay the blame on me,'
    It's a long way, etc.

Molly wrote a neat reply to Irish Paddy O',
Saying 'Mike Maloney wants to marry me, and so
Leave the Strand and Piccadilly, or you'll be to blame,
For love has fairly drove me silly – hoping you're the same!'
    It's a long way, etc.

Jack Judge and Harry Williams, 1912

Pack up your Troubles

Chorus

Hi! Pack up your troubles in your old kit bag,
And smile, smile, smile.
While you've a lucifer to light your fag,
Smile, boys, that's the style.
What's the use of worrying?
It never was worth while, so
Pack up your troubles in your old kit bag,
And smile, smile, smile.

George Asaf, 1915

Take me back to Dear Old Blighty

Chorus

Take me back to dear old Blighty,
Put me on the train for London Town.
Take me over there, drop me anywhere –
Liverpool, Leeds or Birmingham, well I don't care!
I should love to see my best girl,
Cuddling up again we soon should be;
Whoa! Tiddley iddley ighty, hurry me home to Blighty;
Blighty is the place for me.

A.J. Mills, Fred Godfrey and Bennett Scott, 1916

Keep the Home Fires Burning

They were summoned from the hillside,
They were called in from the glen,
And the Country found them ready
At the stirring call for men.
Let no tears add to their hardship,
As the soldiers pass along,
And although your heart is breaking
Make it sing this cheery song.
　　Keep the home fires burning,
　　While your hearts are yearning,
　　Though your lads are far away
　　They dream of Home;
　　There's a silver lining
　　Through the dark cloud shining.
　　Turn the dark cloud inside out,
　　Till the boys come home.

Over seas there came a pleading,
'Help a nation in distress!'
And we gave our glorious laddies;
Honour bade us do no less.
For no gallant Son of Britain
To a foreign yoke shall bend,
And no Englishman is silent
To the sacred call of Friend.
　　Keep the home fires burning, etc.

Lena Guilbert Ford (to music by Ivor Novello), 1919

Bless 'Em All

They say there's a troopship leaving Bombay,
Bound for Old Blighty's shore,
Heavily laden with time-expired men,
Bound for the land they adore.
There's many an airman just finishing his time,
There's many a twirp signing on.
You'll get no promotion this side of the ocean,
So cheer up, my lads, bless 'em all.
   Bless 'em all! Bless 'em all!
   The long and the short and the tall;
   Bless all the sergeants and W.O.1.s,
   Bless all the corp'rals and their blinkin' sons,
   'Cos we're saying goodbye to them all
   As back to their billets they crawl.
   You'll get no promotion this side of the ocean,
   So cheer up, my lads, bless 'em all!
   (*last time*) Nobody knows what a twirp you've been,
   So cheer up, my lads, bless 'em all!

They say, if you work hard you'll get better pay,
We've heard it all before,
Clean up your buttons and polish your boots,
Scrub out the barrack-room floor.
There's many a rookie has taken it in,
Hook, line and sinker an' all.
You'll get no promotion this side of the ocean,
So cheer up, my lads, bless 'em all!
   Bless 'em all! etc.

Written and composed by Jimmy Hughes and Frank Lake, 1940

The White Cliffs of Dover

I'll never forget the people I met
Braving those angry skies;
I remember well as the shadows fell,
The light of hope in their eyes.
And tho' I'm far away,
I still can hear them say, 'Thumbs up!'
For when the dawn comes up:
    There'll be bluebirds over the white cliffs of Dover
    Tomorrow, just you wait and see.
    There'll be love and laughter and peace ever after,
    Tomorrow, when the world is free.

The shepherd will tend his sheep,
The valley will bloom again,
And Jimmy will go to sleep,
In his own little room again.
    There'll be bluebirds over, etc.

I may not be near, but I have no fear,
Hist'ry will prove it too,
When the tale is told 'twill be as of old
For truth will always win through;
But be I far or near,
That slogan still I'll hear, 'Thumbs up!'
For when the dawn comes up:
    There'll be bluebirds over, etc.

Nat Burton, 1941

The Anglican hymn is a glorious and distinctively British contribution to the world's stock of vocal music. Its first flowering in the eighteenth century was in the Evangelical movement or outside the C of E in Methodist chapels; this was the time of Watts, Wesley, Toplady and Newton. But the period of greatest profusion lasted from the earlier to the late nineteenth century. Neither the writers nor the composers are usually remembered for anything outside the field, and yet many of their creations are small masterpieces, eloquent, straightforward words of praise or appeal fittingly set to vigorous, memorable tunes. Some of those words, like the middle verses of Bishop Heber's magnificent poem, 'From Greenland's icy mountains', have an antiquated ring today, but the tunes have held up, and the four-part settings are still more than fun to sing. Anybody is the poorer who has not at some time in life regularly sung hymns in choir or congregation.

Such is the power of a good tune that it can not only obscure but even transform the meaning of the words. Those of the poem of Blake usually known as 'Jerusalem' are admittedly not the most clear-cut in the world. Nevertheless what the bow and the arrows of desire and the spear are up to in any Christian context is mystifying, and second thoughts eked out with a little knowledge of the poet and his other writings suggest that the paradise he called for was not one of religion or justice but of sexual freedom. Further inquiry makes it very probable that the dark satanic mills, which sound so much like something to do with the Industrial Revolution, and give the congregation a pleasant 'progressive' thrill in the singing, referred in Blake's phraseology to church altars. And yet Parry's powerful setting was for many years enthusiastically roared out not only in church but at school prizegivings, gatherings of the Tory faithful and the like. In the words of the great F.W. Bateson on this phenomenon, 'Will no one tell them what they sing?'

In the last twenty years attempts have been made to accommodate what are often uncompromising hymns or parts of hymns to liberal sentiment. In the course of singing 'For all the saints' at a wedding lately, one of us found himself presented with words that went 'Jesus leads forth against sin's battle-line' (or some such gabble) where in his youth he had been used to 'We feebly struggle, they [i.e. the saints] in glory shine.'

Whether anybody likes it or not, one of the main things about saints is that they are much, much better people than you or me, and until they are declared unacceptably élitist and officially abolished it will do no harm to leave them as they have always been.

The Coventry Carol

Lully, lullay, thou little tiny child,
  By by, lully lullay.

O sisters too,
How may we do
  For to preserve this day
This poor youngling,
For whom we do sing,
  By by, lully lullay?

Herod, the king,
In his raging,
  Chargèd he hath this day
His men of might,
In his own sight,
  All young childrèn to slay.

That woe is me,
Poor child for thee!
  And ever morn and day,
For thy parting
Neither say nor sing
  By by, lully lullay!

Version by Robert Croo, 1534

The Holly and the Ivy

The holly and the ivy,
  When they are both full grown,
Of all the trees that are in the wood
  The holly bears the crown.
    The rising of the sun
    And the running of the deer,
    The playing of the merry organ,
    Sweet singing in the choir.

The holly bears a blossom
  As white as the lily flower,
And Mary bore sweet Jesus Christ
  To be our sweet saviour.
    The rising of the sun, etc.

The holly bears a berry
  As red as any blood,
And Mary bore sweet Jesus Christ
  To do poor sinners good.
    The rising of the sun, etc.

The holly bears a prickle
  As sharp as any thorn,
And Mary bore sweet Jesus Christ
  On Christmas day in the morn.
    The rising of the sun, etc.

The holly bears a bark
  As bitter as any gall,
And Mary bore sweet Jesus Christ
  For to redeem us all.
    The rising of the sun, etc.

The holly and the ivy,
  When they are both full grown,
Of all the trees that are in the wood
  The holly bears the crown.
    The rising of the sun, etc.

Anon., 15th century

I Saw Three Ships

I saw three ships come sailing in,
   On Christmas Day, on Christmas Day,
I saw three ships come sailing in,
   On Christmas Day in the morning.

And what was in those ships all three?
   On Christmas Day, etc.

Our Saviour Christ and his lady.
   On Christmas Day, etc.

Pray, whither sailed those ships all three?
   On Christmas Day, etc.

O, they sailed into Bethlehem.
   On Christmas Day, etc.

And all the bells on earth shall ring,
   On Christmas Day, etc.

And all the angels in Heaven shall sing.
   On Christmas Day, etc.

And all the souls on earth shall sing.
   On Christmas Day, etc.

Then let us all rejoice amain!
   On Christmas Day, etc.

Anon.

The Wassail Song

Here we come a-wassailing
    Among the leaves so green,
Here we come a-wandering,
    So fair to be seen:
        Love and joy come to you,
        And to you your wassail too,
        And God bless you, and send you
        A happy new year.

Our wassail cup is made
    Of the rosemary tree,
And so is your beer
    Of the best barley:
        Love and joy, etc.

We are not daily beggars
    That beg from door to door,
But we are neighbours' children
    Whom you have seen before:
        Love and joy, etc.

Call up the butler of this house,
    Put on his golden ring;
Let him bring us up a glass of beer,
    And better we shall sing:
        Love and joy, etc.

We have got a little purse
    Of stretching leather skin;
We want a little of your money
    To line it well within:
        Love and joy, etc.

Bring us out a table,
    And spread it with a cloth;
Bring us out a mouldy cheese,
    And some of your Christmas loaf:
        Love and joy, etc.

God bless the master of this house,
    Likewise the mistress too;
And all the little children
    That round the table go:
        Love and joy, etc.

Good Master and good Mistress,
    While you're sitting by the fire,
Pray think of us poor children
    Who are wandering in the mire:
        Love and joy, etc.

Anon.

The First Nowell

The first Nowell the angel did say
Was to certain poor shepherds in fields as they lay;
In fields where they lay, keeping their sheep,
In a cold winter's night that was so deep:
    Nowell, Nowell, Nowell, Nowell,
    Born is the King of Israel!

They lookèd up and saw a star,
Shining in the east, beyond them far;
And to the earth it gave great light,
And so it continued both day and night:
    Nowell, Nowell, etc.

And by the light of that same star,
Three Wise Men came from country far;
To seek for a king was their intent,
And to follow the star wheresoever it went:
    Nowell, Nowell, etc.

This star drew nigh to the north-west;
O'er Bethlehem it took its rest,
And there it did both stop and stay
Right over the place where Jesus lay:
    Nowell, Nowell, etc.

Then did they know assuredly
Within that house the King did lie:
One entered in then for to see,
And found the babe in poverty:
    Nowell, Nowell, etc.

Then entered in those Wise Men three,
Fell reverently upon their knee,
And offered there in his presènce
Both gold and myrrh and frankincense:
    Nowell, Nowell, etc.

Between an ox-stall and an ass
This child truly there born he was;
For want of clothing they did him lay
All in the manger, among the hay:
    Nowell, Nowell, etc.

Then let us all with one accord
Sing praises to our heavenly Lord,
That hath made heaven and earth of naught,
And with his blood mankind hath bought:
    Nowell, Nowell, etc.

If we in our time shall do well,
We shall be free from death and hell;
For God hath prepared for us all
A resting place in general:
    Nowell, Nowell, etc.

Anon.

God Rest you Merry, Gentlemen

God rest you merry, gentlemen,
  Let nothing you dismay,
Remember Christ our Saviour
  Was born on Christmas Day,
To save poor souls from Satan's power
  That had long time gone astray,
    O tidings of comfort and joy.

From God that is our Father,
  The blessèd angels came,
Unto some certain shepherds,
  With tidings of the same;
That there was born in Bethlehem,
  The Son of God by name.
    O tidings, etc.

Go, fear not, said God's angels,
  Let nothing you affright,
For there is born in Bethlehem,
  Of a pure Virgin bright,
One able to advance you,
  And throw down Satan quite.
    O tidings, etc.

The shepherds at those tidings,
  Rejoicèd much in mind,
And left their flocks a-feeding
  In tempest storms of wind,
And strait they came to Bethlehem,
  The Son of God to find.
    O tidings, etc.

Now when they came to Bethlehem,
  Where our sweet Saviour lay,
They found Him in a manger,
  Where oxen feed on hay,
The blessèd Virgin kneeling down,
  Unto the Lord did pray.
    O tidings, etc.

With sudden joy and gladness,
  The shepherds were beguil'd,
To see the Babe of Israel,
  Before his mother mild,
On them with joy and cheerfulness,
  Rejoice each mother's child.
    O tidings, etc.

Now to the Lord sing praises,
  All you within this place,
Like we true loving brethren,
  Each other to embrace,
For the merry time of Christmas,
  Is drawing on apace.
    O tidings, etc.

God bless the ruler of this house,
  And send him long to reign,
And many a merry Christmas
  May live to see again.
Among your friends and kindred,
  That live both far and near,
    And God send you a happy New Year.

Anon.

47

While Shepherds Watched

While shepherds watched their flocks by night,
   All seated on the ground,
The Angel of the Lord came down,
   And glory shone around.
'Fear not,' said he (for mighty dread
   Had seized their troubled mind);
'Glad tidings of great joy I bring
   To you and all mankind.

'To you in David's town this day
   Is born of David's line
A Saviour, who is Christ the Lord;
   And this shall be the sign:
The heavenly Babe you there shall find
   To human view displayed,
All meanly wrapped in swathing bands,
   And in a manger laid.'

Thus spake the Seraph: and forthwith
   Appeared a shining throng
Of angels praising God, who thus
   Addressed their joyful song:
'All glory be to God on high,
   And to the earth be peace;
Good-will henceforth from heaven to men
   Begin and never cease.'

Nahum Tate 1652–1715

Hark, the Herald Angels Sing

Hark! the herald-angels sing
Glory to the new-born King,
Peace on earth, and mercy mild,
God and sinners reconciled.
Joyful, all ye nations, rise,
Join the triumph of the skies;
With the Angelic host proclaim,
'Christ is born in Bethlehem.'
   Hark! the herald-angels sing
   Glory to the new-born King.

Christ, by highest Heav'n adored,
Christ, the Everlasting Lord,
Late in time behold Him come,
Offspring of a Virgin's womb.
Veil'd in flesh the Godhead see!
Hail, the Incarnate Deity!
Pleased as Man with man to dwell.
Jesus, our Emmanuel.
   Hark! the herald-angels sing
   Glory to the new-born King.

Hail, the heaven-born Prince of peace!
Hail, the Sun of righteousness!
Light and life to all He brings,
Risen with healing in His wings.
Mild He lays His glory by,
Born that man no more may die,
Born to raise the sons of earth,
Born to give them second birth.
   Hark! the herald-angels sing
   Glory to the new-born King.

Charles Wesley 1707–1788

Good King Wenceslas

Good King Wenceslas looked out,
  On the Feast of Stephen,
When the snow lay round about,
  Deep, and crisp, and even:
Brightly shone the moon that night,
  Though the frost was cruel,
When a poor man came in sight,
  Gathering winter fuel.

'Hither, page, and stand by me,
  If thou know'st it, telling,
Yonder peasant, who is he?
  Where and what his dwelling?'
'Sire, he lives a good league hence,
  Underneath the mountain,
Right against the forest fence,
  By Saint Agnes' fountain.'

'Bring me flesh, and bring me wine,
  Bring me pine-logs hither:
Thou and I will see him dine,
  When we bear them thither.'
Page and monarch, forth they went,
  Forth they went together:
Through the rude wind's wild lament
  And the bitter weather.

'Sire, the night is darker now,
  And the wind blows stronger;
Fails my heart, I know not how;
  I can go no longer.'
'Mark my footsteps, good my page;
  Tread thou in them boldly:
Thou shalt find the winter's rage
  Freeze thy blood less coldly.'

In his master's steps he trod,
  Where the snow lay dinted;
Heat was in the very sod
  Which the Saint had printed.
Therefore, Christian men, be sure,
  Wealth or rank possessing,
Ye who now will bless the poor,
  Shall yourselves find blessing.

J.M. Neale 1818–1866

In the Bleak Mid-Winter

In the bleak mid-winter
   Frosty wind made moan,
Earth stood hard as iron,
   Water like a stone;
Snow had fallen, snow on snow,
   Snow on snow,
In the bleak mid-winter,
   Long ago.

Our God, heaven cannot hold him
   Nor earth sustain;
Heaven and earth shall flee away
   When he comes to reign:
In the bleak mid-winter
   A stable-place sufficed
The Lord God Almighty
   Jesus Christ.

Enough for him, whom Cherubim
   Worship night and day,
A breastful of milk,
   And a mangerful of hay;
Enough for him, whom Angels
   Fall down before,
The ox and ass and camel
   Which adore.

Angels and Archangels
   May have gathered there,
Cherubim and Seraphim
   Thronged the air:
But only his mother
   In her maiden bliss
Worshipped the Beloved
   With a kiss.

What can I give him,
   Poor as I am?
If I were a shepherd
   I would bring a lamb;
If I were a wise man
   I would do my part;
Yet what I can I give him –
   Give my heart.

Christina Rossetti 1830–1894

O Little Town of Bethlehem

O little town of Bethlehem,
    How still we see thee lie!
Above thy deep and dreamless sleep
    The silent stars go by.
Yet in thy dark streets shineth
    The everlasting light;
The hopes and fears of all the years
    Are met in thee to-night.

O morning stars, together
    Proclaim the holy birth,
And praises sing to God the King,
    And peace to men on earth;
For Christ is born of Mary;
    And, gathered all above,
While mortals sleep, the angels keep
    Their watch of wondering love.

How silently, how silently,
    The wondrous gift is given!
So God imparts to human hearts
    The blessings of his heaven.
No ear may hear his coming;
    But in this world of sin,
Where meek souls will receive him, still
    The dear Christ enters in.

Where children pure and happy
    Pray to the blessed Child,
Where misery cries out to thee,
    Son of the mother mild;
Where charity stands watching
    And faith holds wide the door,
The dark night wakes, the glory breaks,
    And Christmas comes once more.

O holy Child of Bethlehem,
    Descend to us, we pray;
Cast out our sin, and enter in,
    Be born in us to-day.
We hear the Christmas Angels
    The great glad tidings tell:
O come to us, abide with us,
    Our Lord Emmanuel.

Bishop Phillips Brooks 1835–1893

Once in Royal David's City

Once in royal David's city
   Stood a lowly cattle shed,
Where a Mother laid her Baby
   In a manger for His bed;
Mary was that Mother mild,
Jesus Christ her little Child.

He came down to earth from Heaven
   Who is God and Lord of all,
And His shelter was a stable,
   And His cradle was a stall;
With the poor, and mean, and lowly,
Lived on earth our Saviour Holy.

And, through all His wondrous Childhood,
   He would honour and obey,
Love, and watch the lowly Maiden,
   In whose gentle arms He lay;
Christian children all must be
Mild, obedient, good as He.

For He is our childhood's pattern.
   Day by day like us He grew,
He was little, weak, and helpless,
   Tears and smiles like us He knew;
And He feeleth for our sadness,
And He shareth in our gladness.

And our eyes at last shall see Him,
   Through His own redeeming love,
For that Child so dear and gentle
   Is our Lord in Heav'n above;
And He leads His children on
To the place where He is gone.

Not in that poor lowly stable,
   With the oxen standing by,
We shall see Him; but in Heaven,
   Set at God's right hand on high;
When like stars His children crown'd
All in white shall wait around.

Cecil Frances Alexander 1823–1895

All People that on Earth do Dwell

All people that on earth do dwell,
　Sing to the Lord with cheerful voice;
Him serve with mirth, his praise forth tell,
　Come ye before him, and rejoice.

The Lord, ye know, is God indeed;
　Without our aid he did us make;
We are his folk, he doth us feed,
　And for his sheep he doth us take.

O enter then his gates with praise;
　Approach with joy his courts unto;
Praise, laud, and bless his name always,
　For it is seemly so to do.

For why, the Lord our God is good:
　His mercy is for ever sure;
His truth at all times firmly stood,
　And shall from age to age endure.

To Father, Son, and Holy Ghost,
　The God whom heaven and earth adore,
From men and from the angel-host
　Be praise and glory evermore.

William Kethe (d. 1608)

The Lord's my Shepherd

The Lord's my shepherd, I'll not want.
He makes me down to lie
In pastures green; he leadeth me
The quiet waters by.
My soul he doth restore again;
And me to walk doth make
Within the paths of righteousness,
Ev'n for his own name's sake.

Yea, though I walk in death's dark vale,
Yet will I fear none ill:
For thou art with me; and thy rod
And staff me comfort still.
My table thou hast furnishèd
In presence of my foes;
My head thou dost with oil anoint,
And my cup overflows.

Scottish Metrical Psalms, 1650

To Be a Pilgrim

He who would valiant be
   'Gainst all disaster,
Let him in constancy
   Follow the Master.
There's no discouragement
Shall make him once relent
His first avowed intent
   To be a pilgrim.

Who so beset him round
   With dismal stories,
Do but themselves confound –
   His strength the more is.
No foes shall stay his might,
Though he with giants fight:
He will make good his right
   To be a pilgrim.

Since, Lord, thou dost defend
   Us with thy Spirit,
We know we at the end
   Shall life inherit.
Then fancies flee away!
I'll fear not what men say,
I'll labour night and day
   To be a pilgrim.

John Bunyan 1628–1688

O God, our Help in Ages Past

O God, our help in ages past,
  Our hope for years to come,
Our shelter from the stormy blast,
  And our eternal home;

Under the shadow of thy throne
  Thy saints have dwelt secure;
Sufficient is thine arm alone,
  And our defence is sure.

Before the hills in order stood,
  Or earth received her frame,
From everlasting thou art God,
  To endless years the same.

A thousand ages in thy sight
  Are like an evening gone,
Short as the watch that ends the night
  Before the rising sun.

Time, like an ever-rolling stream,
  Bears all its sons away;
They fly forgotten, as a dream
  Dies at the opening day.

O God, our help in ages past,
  Our hope for years to come,
Be thou our guard while troubles last,
  And our eternal home.

Isaac Watts 1674–1748

When I Survey the Wondrous Cross

When I survey the wondrous cross,
   On which the Prince of Glory died,
My richest gain I count but loss,
   And pour contempt on all my pride.

Forbid it, Lord, that I should boast
   Save in the death of Christ my God;
All the vain things that charm me most,
   I sacrifice them to his blood.

See from his head, his hands, his feet,
   Sorrow and love flow mingled down;
Did e'er such love and sorrow meet,
   Or thorns compose so rich a crown?

His dying crimson, like a robe,
   Spreads o'er his body on the tree;
Then am I dead to all the globe,
   And all the globe is dead to me.

Were the whole realm of nature mine,
   That were a present far too small;
Love so amazing, so divine,
   Demands my soul, my life, my all.

Isaac Watts 1674–1748

Guide Me, O Thou Great Redeemer

Guide me, O Thou great Redeemer,
  Pilgrim through this barren land;
I am weak, but Thou art mighty,
  Hold me with Thy powerful hand;
    Bread of Heaven,
Feed me now and evermore.

Open now the crystal fountain,
  Whence the healing streams do flow:
Let the fiery cloudy pillar
  Lead me all my journey through;
    Strong Deliverer,
Be Thou still my Strength and Shield.

When I tread the verge of Jordan,
  Bid my anxious fears subside:
Death of death, and hell's Destruction,
  Land me safe on Canaan's side:
    Songs of praises
I will ever give to Thee.

William Williams 1717–1791

Love Divine, All Loves Excelling

Love Divine, all loves excelling,
   Joy of Heav'n, to earth come down,
Fix in us Thy humble dwelling,
   All Thy faithful mercies crown.
Jesu, Thou art all compassion,
   Pure unbounded love Thou art;
Visit us with Thy salvation,
   Enter every trembling heart.

Come, Almighty to deliver,
   Let us all Thy grace receive;
Suddenly return, and never,
   Never more Thy temples leave.
Thee we would be always blessing,
   Serve Thee as Thy Hosts above;
Pray, and praise Thee, without ceasing,
   Glory in Thy perfect love.

Finish then Thy new creation,
   Pure and spotless let us be;
Let us see Thy great salvation,
   Perfectly restored in Thee.
Changed from glory into glory,
   Till in Heav'n we take our place,
Till we cast our crowns before Thee,
   Lost in wonder, love, and praise.

Charles Wesley 1707–1788

Rock of Ages

Rock of ages, cleft for me,
Let me hide myself in Thee;
Let the water and the blood,
From Thy riven side which flowed,
Be of sin the double cure:
Cleanse me from its guilt and power.

Not the labours of my hands
Can fulfil Thy law's demands;
Could my zeal no respite know,
Could my tears for ever flow,
All for sin could not atone:
Thou must save, and Thou alone.

Nothing in my hand I bring;
Simply to Thy cross I cling;
Naked, come to Thee for dress;
Helpless, look to Thee for grace;
Foul, I to the fountain fly;
Wash me, Saviour, or I die.

While I draw this fleeting breath,
When mine eyes are closed in death,
When I soar through tracts unknown,
See Thee on Thy judgement throne;
Rock of ages, cleft for me,
Let me hide myself in Thee.

A.M. Toplady 1740–1778

Glorious Things of Thee are Spoken

Glorious things of thee are spoken,
   Zion, city of our God;
He Whose word cannot be broken
   Form'd thee for His own abode.
On the Rock of ages founded,
   What can shake thy sure repose?
With salvation's walls surrounded,
   Thou may'st smile at all thy foes.

See, the streams of living waters,
   Springing from eternal love,
Well supply thy sons and daughters,
   And all fear of want remove.
Who can faint while such a river
   Ever flows their thirst to assuage;
Grace, which like the Lord the Giver,
   Never fails from age to age?

Round each habitation hov'ring,
   See the cloud and fire appear,
For a glory and a cov'ring –
   Showing that the Lord is near.
Thus they march, the pillar leading,
   Light by night and shade by day;
Daily on the manna feeding
   Which He gives them when they pray.

Saviour, since of Zion's city
   I, through grace, a member am,
Let the world deride or pity,
   I will glory in Thy Name.
Fading is the world's best pleasure,
   All its boasted pomp and show;
Solid joys and lasting treasure
   None but Zion's children know.

John Newton 1725–1807

Jerusalem

And did those feet in ancient time
Walk upon England's mountains green?
And was the holy Lamb of God
On England's pleasant pastures seen?

And did the Countenance Divine
Shine forth upon our clouded hills?
And was Jerusalem builded here
Among these dark Satanic Mills?

Bring me my Bow of burning gold!
Bring me my Arrows of desire!
Bring me my Spear! O clouds, unfold!
Bring me my Chariot of fire!

I will not cease from Mental Fight,
Nor shall my Sword sleep in my hand,
Till we have built Jerusalem
In England's green and pleasant land.

William Blake 1757–1827

From Greenland's Icy Mountains

From Greenland's icy mountains,
   From India's coral strand,
Where Afric's sunny fountains
   Roll down their golden sand,
From many an ancient river,
   From many a palmy plain,
They call us to deliver
   Their land from error's chain.

What though the spicy breezes
   Blow soft o'er Java's isle,
Though every prospect pleases
   And only man is vile,
In vain with lavish kindness
   The gifts of God are strewn,
The heathen in his blindness
   Bows down to wood and stone.

Can we, whose souls are lighted
   With wisdom from on high,
Can we to men benighted
   The lamp of life deny?
Salvation! oh, salvation!
   The joyful sound proclaim,
Till each remotest nation
   Has learned Messiah's name.

Waft, waft, ye winds, his story,
   And you, ye waters, roll,
Till, like a sea of glory,
   It spreads from pole to pole;
Till o'er our ransomed nature
   The Lamb for sinners slain,
Redeemer, King, Creator,
   In bliss returns to reign.

Reginald Heber 1783–1826

Praise, my Soul, the King of Heaven

Praise, my soul, the King of Heaven,
　To His feet thy tribute bring;
Ransom'd, heal'd, restored, forgiven,
　Evermore His praises sing;
　　Alleluia! Alleluia!
　Praise the everlasting King.

Praise Him for His grace and favour
　To our fathers in distress;
Praise Him still the same as ever,
　Slow to chide, and swift to bless;
　　Alleluia! Alleluia!
　Glorious in His faithfulness.

Father-like, He tends and spares us,
　Well our feeble frame He knows;
In His hands He gently bears us,
　Rescues us from all our foes,
　　Alleluia! Alleluia!
　Widely yet His mercy flows.

Angels in the height, adore Him;
　Ye behold Him face to face;
Saints triumphant, bow before Him,
　Gather'd in from every race;
　　Alleluia! Alleluia!
　Praise with us the God of grace.

H.F. Lyte 1793–1847

Abide with Me

Abide with me; fast falls the eventide;
The darkness deepens; Lord, with me abide.
When other helpers fail, and comforts flee,
Help of the helpless, O abide with me!

Swift to its close ebbs out life's little day;
Earth's joys grow dim, its glories pass away:
Change and decay in all around I see,
O Thou who changest not, abide with me.

Not a brief glance I beg, a passing word;
But as Thou dwelt'st with Thy disciples, Lord,
Familiar, condescending, patient, free, –
Come, not to sojourn, but abide with me.

Come not in terrors, as the King of kings;
But kind and good, with healing in Thy wings,
Tears for all woes, a heart for every plea,
Come, Friend of sinners, and thus bide with me.

Thou on my head in early youth didst smile,
And, though rebellious and perverse meanwhile,
Thou hast not left me, oft as I left Thee,
On to the close, O Lord, abide with me!

I need Thy presence every passing hour;
What but Thy grace can foil the tempter's power?
Who like Thyself my guide and stay can be?
Through cloud and sunshine, Lord, abide with me.

I fear no foe with Thee at hand to bless;
Ills have no weight and tears no bitterness;
Where is death's sting? Where, grave, thy victory?
I triumph still if Thou abide with me.

Hold Thou Thy cross before my closing eyes;
Shine through the gloom and point me to the skies!
Heaven's morning breaks and earth's vain shadows flee;
In life, in death, O Lord, abide with me.

H.F. Lyte 1793–1847

Lead, Kindly Light

Lead, kindly Light, amid the encircling gloom,
    Lead Thou me on;
The night is dark, and I am far from home,
    Lead Thou me on.
Keep Thou my feet; I do not ask to see
The distant scene; one step enough for me.

I was not ever thus, nor prayed that Thou
    Should'st lead me on;
I loved to choose and see my path; but now
    Lead Thou me on.
I loved the garish day, and, spite of fears,
Pride ruled my will: remember not past years.

So long Thy power hath blest me, sure it still
    Will lead me on
O'er moor and fen, o'er crag and torrent, till
    The night is gone,
And with the morn those angel faces smile,
Which I have loved long since, and lost awhile.

Praise to the Holiest

Praise to the Holiest in the height,
    And in the depth be praise;
In all His words most wonderful,
    Most sure in all His ways.

O loving wisdom of our God!
    When all was sin and shame,
A second Adam to the fight
    And to the rescue came.

O wisest love! that flesh and blood,
    Which did in Adam fail,
Should strive afresh against the foe,
    Should strive and should prevail;

And that a higher gift than grace
    Should flesh and blood refine,
God's Presence and His very Self,
    And Essence all-divine.

O generous love! that He, Who smote
    In Man for man the foe,
The double agony in Man
    For man should undergo;

And in the garden secretly,
    And on the Cross on high,
Should teach His brethren, and inspire
    To suffer and to die.

Praise to the Holiest in the height,
    And in the depth be praise;
In all His words most wonderful,
    Most sure in all His ways.

John Henry, Cardinal Newman 1801–1890

We Plough the Fields and Scatter

We plough the fields, and scatter
  The good seed on the land,
But it is fed and watered
  By God's almighty hand:
He sends the snow in winter,
  The warmth to swell the grain,
The breezes and the sunshine,
  And soft refreshing rain:
    All good gifts around us
      Are sent from heaven above;
    Then thank the Lord, O thank the Lord,
      For all His love.

He only is the maker
  Of all things near and far,
He paints the wayside flower,
  He lights the evening star.
The winds and waves obey Him,
  By him the birds are fed;
Much more to us, His children,
  He gives our daily bread:
    All good gifts around us, etc.

We thank thee then, O Father,
  For all things bright and good;
The seed-time and the harvest,
  Our life, our health, our food.
No gifts have we to offer
  For all Thy love imparts,
But that which Thou desirest,
  Our humble, thankful hearts:
    All good gifts around us, etc.

Jane M. Campbell 1817–1878

City of God

City of God, how broad and far
  Outspread thy walls sublime!
The true thy chartered freemen are
  Of every age and clime.

One holy Church, one army strong,
  One steadfast, high intent;
One working band, one harvest-song,
  One King omnipotent.

How purely hath thy speech come down
  From man's primeval youth!
How grandly hath thine empire grown
  Of freedom, love, and truth!

How gleam thy watch-fires through the night
  With never-fainting ray!
How rise thy towers, serene and bright,
  To meet the dawning day!

In vain the surge's angry shock,
  In vain the drifting sands:
Unharmed upon the eternal Rock
  The eternal City stands.

S. Johnson 1822–1882

All Things Bright and Beautiful

All things bright and beautiful,
    All creatures great and small,
All things wise and wonderful,
    The Lord God made them all.

Each little flower that opens,
    Each little bird that sings,
He made their glowing colours,
    He made their tiny wings.

The rich man in his castle,
    The poor man at his gate,
God made them, high or lowly,
    And order'd their estate.

The purple-headed mountain,
    The river running by,
The sunset and the morning,
    That brightens up the sky; –

The cold wind in the winter,
    The pleasant summer sun,
The ripe fruits in the garden, –
    He made them every one;

The tall trees in the greenwood,
    The meadows where we play,
The rushes by the water,
    We gather every day; –

He gave us eyes to see them,
    And lips that we might tell
How great is God Almighty,
    Who has made all things well.

Cecil Frances Alexander 1823–1895

Eternal Father, Strong to Save

Eternal Father, strong to save,
Whose arm doth bind the restless wave,
Who bidd'st the mighty ocean deep
Its own appointed limits keep:
    O hear us when we cry to Thee
    For those in peril on the sea.

O Saviour, Whose almighty word,
The winds and waves submissive heard,
Who walkedst on the foaming deep,
And calm amid its rage didst sleep:
    O hear us when we cry to Thee
    For those in peril on the sea.

O sacred Spirit, who didst brood
Upon the chaos dark and rude,
Who bad'st its angry tumult cease,
And gavest light and life and peace:
    O hear us when we cry to Thee
    For those in peril on the sea.

O Trinity of love and power,
Our brethren shield in danger's hour;
From rock and tempest, fire and foe,
Protect them wheresoe'er they go:
    And ever let there rise to Thee
    Glad hymns of praise from land and sea.

William Whiting 1825–1878

The Day Thou Gavest

The day Thou gavest, Lord, is ended,
　　The darkness falls at Thy behest;
To Thee our morning hymns ascended,
　　Thy praise shall sanctify our rest.

We thank Thee that Thy Church unsleeping,
　　While earth rolls onward into light,
Through all the world her watch is keeping,
　　And rests not now by day or night.

As o'er each continent and island
　　The dawn leads on another day,
The voice of prayer is never silent,
　　Nor dies the strain of praise away.

The sun that bids us rest is waking
　　Our brethren 'neath the western sky,
And hour by hour fresh lips are making
　　Thy wondrous doings heard on high.

So be it, Lord; Thy throne shall never,
　　Like earth's proud empires, pass away;
Thy kingdom stands, and grows for ever,
　　Till all Thy creatures own thy sway.

John Ellerton 1826–1893

Onward, Christian Soldiers

Onward, Christian soldiers!
  Marching as to war,
With the cross of Jesus
  Going on before.
Christ the royal Master
  Leads against the foe;
Forward into battle,
  See, his banners go:
    Onward, Christian soldiers,
      Marching as to war,
      With the cross of Jesus
        Going on before.

At the sign of triumph
  Satan's legions flee;
On then, Christian soldiers,
  On to victory!
Hell's foundations quiver
  At the shout of praise;
Brothers, lift your voices,
  Loud your anthems raise:
    Onward, Christian soldiers, etc.

Like a mighty army
  Moves the Church of God;
Brothers, we are treading
  Where the saints have trod;
We are not divided,
  All one body we,
One in hope and doctrine,
  One in charity:
    Onward, Christian soldiers, etc.

Crowns and thrones may perish,
  Kingdoms rise and wane,
But the Church of Jesus
  Constant will remain;
Gates of hell can never
  'Gainst that Church prevail;
We have Christ's own promise,
  And that cannot fail:
    Onward, Christian soldiers, etc.

Through the Night of Doubt and Sorrow

Through the night of doubt and sorrow
  Onward goes the pilgrim band,
Singing songs of expectation,
  Marching to the Promised Land.

Clear before us through the darkness
  Gleams and burns the guiding light;
Brother clasps the hand of brother,
  Stepping fearless through the night.

One the light of God's own presence
  O'er his ransomed people shed,
Chasing far the gloom and terror,
  Brightening all the path we tread;

One the object of our journey,
  One the faith which never tires,
One the earnest looking forward,
  One the hope our God inspires:

One the strain that lips of thousands
  Lift as from the heart of one;
One the conflict, one the peril,
  One the march in God begun;

One the gladness of rejoicing
  On the far eternal shore,
Where the one almighty Father
  Reigns in love for evermore.

Sabine Baring-Gould 1834–1924

72

As with Gladness Men of Old

As with gladness men of old
Did the guiding star behold,
As with joy they hailed its light,
Leading onward, beaming bright,
So, most gracious God, may we
Evermore be led to Thee.

As with joyful steps they sped
To that lowly manger-bed,
There to bend the knee before
Him whom heaven and earth adore,
So may we with willing feet
Ever seek Thy mercy-seat.

As they offered gifts most rare
At that manger rude and bare,
So may we with holy joy,
Pure, and free from sin's alloy,
All our costliest treasures bring,
Christ, to Thee our heavenly King.

Holy Jesus, every day
Keep us in the narrow way;
And, when earthly things are past,
Bring our ransomed souls at last
Where they need no star to guide,
Where no clouds Thy glory hide.

In the heavenly country bright
Need they no created light;
Thou its light, its joy, its crown,
Thou its sun which goes not down:
There for ever may we sing
Alleluyas to our King.

W. Chatterton Dix 1837–1898

73

For all the Saints

For all the Saints who from their labours rest,
Who Thee by faith before the world confessed,
Thy name, O Jesu, be for ever blessed,
Alleluya!

Thou wast their Rock, their Fortress and their Might;
Thou, Lord, their Captain in the well-fought fight;
Thou in the darkness drear their one true Light.
Alleluya!

O may Thy soldiers, faithful, true, and bold,
Fight as the Saints who nobly fought of old,
And win, with them, the victor's crown of gold.
Alleluya!

O blest communion! fellowship Divine!
We feebly struggle, they in glory shine;
Yet all are one in Thee, for all are Thine.
Alleluya!

And when the strife is fierce, the warfare long,
Steals on the ear the distant triumph song,
And hearts are brave again, and arms are strong.
Alleluya!

The golden evening brightens in the west;
Soon, soon to faithful warriors comes their rest;
Sweet is the calm of Paradise the blest.
Alleluya!

But lo! there breaks a yet more glorious day;
The Saints triumphant rise in bright array:
The King of glory passes on His way.
Alleluya!

From earth's wide bounds, from ocean's farthest coast,
Through gates of pearl streams in the countless host,
Singing to Father, Son, and Holy Ghost.
Alleluya!

Bishop W. Walsham How 1823–1897

74

The King of Love my Shepherd is

The King of love my Shepherd is,
   Whose goodness faileth never;
I nothing lack if I am His
   And He is mine for ever.

Where streams of living water flow
   My ransom'd soul He leadeth,
And, where the verdant pastures grow,
   With food celestial feedeth.

Perverse and foolish oft I stray'd,
   But yet in love He sought me,
And on His shoulder gently laid,
   And home, rejoicing, brought me.

In death's dark vale I fear no ill
   With Thee, dear Lord, beside me;
Thy rod and staff my comfort still,
   Thy Cross before to guide me.

Thou spread'st a Table in my sight;
   Thy Unction grace bestoweth;
And oh, what transport of delight
   From Thy pure Chalice floweth!

And so through all the length of days
   Thy goodness faileth never:
Good Shepherd, may I sing Thy praise
   Within Thy house for ever.

Sir H.W. Baker 1821–1877

Joshua Fit de Battle of Jerico

Joshua fit de battle of Jerico,
Jerico, Jerico,
Joshua fit de battle of Jerico,
An' de walls come tumblin' down.

You may talk about yo' king of Gideon,
You may talk about yo' man of Saul,
Dere's none like good ol' Joshua
At de battle of Jerico.

Up to de walls of Jerico
He marched with spear in han'
'Go blow dem ram horns,' Joshua cried,
'Cause de battle am in my han'.'

Den de lam'ram sheep horns begin to blow,
Trumpets begin to soun',
Joshua commanded de chillen to shout,
An' de walls come tumblin' down.

Dat mornin' Joshua fit de battle of Jerico,
Jerico, Jerico,
Joshua fit de battle of Jerico,
An' de walls come tumblin' down.

Anon.

All God's Chillun Got Wings

I got a robe, you got a robe,
All o' God's chillun got a robe.
When I get to Heaven I'm goin' to put on my robe,
I'm goin' to shout all over God's Heaven,
    Heaven, Heaven,
    Everybody talkin' 'bout Heaven ain't goin' there,
    Heaven, Heaven,
    I'm goin' to shout all over God's Heaven.

I got-a wings, you got-a wings,
All o' God's chillun got-a wings.
When I get to Heaven I'm goin' to put on my wings,
I'm goin' to fly all over God's Heaven,
    Heaven, Heaven, etc.
    I'm goin' to fly all over God's Heaven.

I got a harp, you got a harp,
All o' God's chillun got a harp.
When I get to Heaven I'm goin' to take up my harp,
I'm goin' to play all over God's Heaven,
    Heaven, Heaven, etc.
    I'm goin' to play all over God's Heaven.

I got shoes, you got shoes,
All God's chillun got shoes.
When I get to Heaven I'm goin' to put on my shoes,
I'm goin' to walk all over God's Heaven.
    Heaven, Heaven,
    Everybody talkin' 'bout Heaven ain't goin' there,
    Heaven, Heaven,
    I'm goin' to walk all over God's Heaven,
    I'm goin' to walk all over God's Heaven,
    I'm goin' to walk all over God's Heaven,
    I'm going to walk all over, goin' to talk all over God's Heaven.

Anon.

Swing Low, Sweet Chariot

Swing low, sweet chariot,
Comin' for to carry me home,
Swing low, sweet chariot,
Comin' for to carry me home.

I looked over Jordan, and what did I see,
Comin' for to carry me home,
A band of angels comin' after me,
Comin' for to carry me home.
   Swing low, sweet chariot, etc.

If you get there before I do,
Comin' for to carry me home,
Tell all my friends I'm comin' too,
Comin' for to carry me home.
   Swing low, sweet chariot, etc.

Anon.

LOVE

Comin' through the rye

Most love poetry in the ordinary sense of the phrase is not appropriate for being used as the basis for song, and English poets have not written regularly for the voice since Tudor times. What was for many years its predominant form, the sonnet, cannot be turned into symmetrical melodic portions. It fades quickly, too, coming to seem strained or unnatural to following generations. Once in a way, a poem has been artificially preserved, so to speak, by being set to a memorable tune. Ben Jonson's lyric 'To Celia' has had this good luck, though the tune we now sing is not the original one, dating as it does from the mid-eighteenth century. Seeing it on the page enhances its elegance and ingenuity, but reveals its extravagance of expression and the sleight-of-hand whereby the seventh and eighth lines are made to seem to mean the opposite of what they say.

Burns is the only British poet of stature to have often written of love in a strong, clear, vivid way and to have done so in poetic forms altogether suitable for setting to melodies equally straightforward, a feat or series of feats probably impossible for an Englishman and certainly never matched by one. 'O, My Luve is like a Red, Red Rose' and 'John Anderson my Jo' are treasured all over the English-speaking world and beyond not only because they are fine but also because they are rare.

Apart from a few isolated successes like 'Come into the Garden, Maud', which most likely owes its place more to its innocent sentimentality than to any note of ardour, British love-songs have tended to come out of the lower social strata. Some would connect this with what it is not hard to see as their greater realism and appeal to common experience when compared with the love poetry mentioned above. Indeed, 'Sally in our Alley' and even 'My Old Dutch' very likely do describe a much larger fraction of day-to-day life than 'Maud' or 'Song to Silvia', though that is not the last word to be said on the subject.

From its origins in folk-song and ballad the British love-song began to move to theatrical entertainments and, in Victorian times, the music-hall. The so-called drawing-room ballad, a type of solo song immensely popular in the fifty years before 1914, sounds a little more elevated, and there is genteel language in such as 'I'll Sing thee Songs of Araby' and 'Because', but in most cases the drawing-room would have been aspired to rather than real. The musical evening, at which groups of friends met informally and took turns to sing, kept some ballads alive until 1939. By that time the availability and acceptance of entertainment by outsiders via gramophone and wireless had seen to it that the ability to accompany such songs at the piano, once very widespread, was becoming rare. If a youngster learned the piano then it was to play Beethoven or Fats Waller.

Greensleeves

Alas, my Love! ye do me wrong
  To cast me off discourteously;
And I have lovèd you so long,
  Delighting in your company.
    Greensleeves was all my joy,
     Greensleeves was my delight;
    Greensleeves was my heart of gold,
     And who but Lady Greensleeves.

I have been ready at your hand,
  To grant whatever you would crave;
I have both wagèd life and land,
  Your love and goodwill for to have,
    Greensleeves was all my joy, etc.

I bought thee kerchers to thy head,
  That were wrought fine and gallantly;
I kept thee both at board and bed,
  Which cost my purse well favouredly.
    Greensleeves was all my joy, etc.

I bought thee petticoats of the best,
  The cloth so fine as fine might be;
I gave thee jewels for thy chest,
  And all this cost I spent on thee.
    Greensleeves was all my joy, etc.

Thy purse and eke thy gay gilt knives,
  Thy pincase gallant to the eye;
No better wore the burgess wives,
  And yet thou wouldst not love me.
    Greensleeves was all my joy, etc.

Thy gown was of the grassy green,
  Thy sleeves of satin hanging by,
Which made thee be our harvest queen,
  And yet thou wouldst not love me.
    Greensleeves was all my joy, etc.

My gayest gelding I thee gave,
  To ride wherever liked thee;
No lady ever was so brave,
  And yet thou wouldst not love me.
    Greensleeves was all my joy, etc.

My men were clothèd all in green,
  And they did ever wait on thee;
All this was gallant to be seen,
  And yet thou wouldst not love me.
    Greensleeves was all my joy, etc.

For every morning when thou rose,
  I sent thee dainties orderly,
To cheer thy stomach from all woes,
  And yet thou wouldst not love me.
    Greensleeves was all my joy, etc.

Well, I will pray to God on high,
  That thou my constancy mayst see,
And that yet once before I die,
  Thou wilt vouchsafe to love me.
    Greensleeves was all my joy, etc.

Greensleeves, now farewell! adieu!
  God I pray to prosper thee;
For I am still thy lover true.
  Come once again and love me.
    Greensleeves was all my joy, etc.

Anon., 1584

Song to Silvia

from *Two Gentlemen of Verona*

Who is Silvia? what is she,
    That all our swains commend her?
Holy, fair, and wise is she;
    The heavens such grace did lend her,
That she might admirèd be.

Is she kind as she is fair?
    For beauty lives with kindness.
Love doth to her eyes repair,
    To help him of his blindness;
And, being helped, inhabits there.

Then to Silvia let us sing,
    That Silvia is excelling;
She excels each mortal thing
    Upon the dull earth dwelling;
To her let us garlands bring.

It Was a Lover and his Lass

The Pages' Song, from *As You Like It*

It was a lover and his lass,
    With a hey, and a ho, and a hey nonino,
That o'er the green corn-field did pass,
    In spring time, the only pretty ring time,
When birds do sing, hey ding a ding, ding;
Sweet lovers love the spring.

Between the acres of the rye,
    With a hey, and a ho, and a hey nonino,
Those pretty country folks would lie,
    In spring time, the only pretty ring time,
When birds do sing, hey ding a ding, ding;
Sweet lovers love the spring.

This carol they began that hour,
    With a hey, and a ho, and a hey nonino,
How that a life was but a flower
    In spring time, the only pretty ring time,
When birds to sing, hey ding a ding, ding;
Sweet lovers love the spring.

And therefore take the present time,
    With a hey, and a ho, and a hey nonino;
For love is crownèd with the prime
    In spring time, the only pretty ring time,
When birds do sing, hey ding a ding, ding;
Sweet lovers love the spring.

William Shakespeare 1564–1616

O Mistress Mine

Feste's Song, from *Twelfth Night*

O mistress mine, where are you roaming?
O! stay and hear; your true love's coming,
   That can sing both high and low.
Trip no further, pretty sweeting;
Journeys end in lovers meeting,
   Every wise man's son doth know.

What is love? 'Tis not hereafter;
Present mirth hath present laughter;
   What's to come is still unsure.
In delay there lies no plenty;
Then come kiss me, sweet and twenty;
   Youth's a stuff will not endure.

William Shakespeare 1564–1616

To Celia

Drink to me only with thine eyes,
   And I will pledge with mine;
Or leave a kiss but in the cup
   And I'll not look for wine.
The thirst that from the soul doth rise
   Doth ask a drink divine;
But might I of Jove's nectar sup,
   I would not change for thine.

I sent thee late a rosy wreath,
   Not so much honouring thee
As giving it a hope that there
   It could not wither'd be;
But thou thereon didst only breathe,
   And sent'st it back to me;
Since when it grows, and smells, I swear,
   Not of itself but thee!

Ben Jonson 1572–1637

Lullaby

Golden slumbers kiss your eyes;
Smiles awake you when you rise.
Sleep, pretty wantons, do not cry,
And I will sing a lullaby:
   Rock them, rock them, lullaby.

Care is heavy, therefore sleep you;
You are care, and care must keep you.
Sleep, pretty wantons, do not cry,
And I will sing a lullaby:
   Rock them, rock them, lullaby.

Thomas Dekker c. 1572–1632

There is a Lady Sweet and Kind

There is a lady sweet and kind,
Was never face so pleased my mind.
I did but see her passing by,
And yet I love her till I die.

Her gesture, motion and her smiles,
Her wit, her voice my heart beguiles,
Beguiles my heart, I know not why,
And yet I love her till I die.

Cupid is wingèd and doth range,
Her country so my love doth change;
But change the earth, or change the sky,
Yet will I love her till I die.

Thomas Ford?–1648

Barbara Allen

In Scarlet Town, where I was born,
    There was a fair maid dwellin',
Made every youth cry 'Well a day!'
    Her name was Barbara Allen.

All in the merry month of May,
    When green buds they were swellin',
Young Jemmy Grove on his death-bed lay
    For love of Barbara Allen.

He sent his man unto her then,
    To the town where she was dwellin', –
'You must come to my master dear,
    If your name be Barbara Allen.'

So slowly, slowly she came up,
    And slowly she came nigh him;
And all she said, when there she came, –
    'Young man, I think you're dying.'

He turn'd his face unto the wall,
    As deadly pangs he fell in;
'Adieu! adieu! adieu to all, –
    Adieu to Barbara Allen!'

When he was dead, and laid in grave,
    Her heart was struck with sorrow:
'O mother, mother, make my bed,
    For I shall die to-morrow!'

She, on her death-bed, as she lay,
    Begg'd to be buried by him,
And sore repented of the day
    That she did e'er deny him.

'Farewell,' she said, 'ye virgins all,
    And shun the fault I fell in;
Henceforth take warning by the fall
    Of cruel Barbara Allen.'

Anon.

O Waly, Waly up the Bank

O waly, waly up the bank,
   And waly, waly down the brae,
And waly, waly yon burn-side,
   Where I and my love wont to gae.

I lean'd my back unto an aik,
   I thought it was a trusty tree,
But first it bow'd, and syne it brak,
   Sae my true-love did lightly me.

O waly, waly, but love be bonny
   A little time, while it is new,
But when 'tis auld it waxeth cauld,
   And fades away like morning dew.

O wherefore should I busk my head?
   Or wherefore should I kame my hair?
For my true-love has me forsook,
   And says he will never love me mair.

Now Arthur-Seat shall be my bed,
   The sheets shall n'er by fyl'd by me;
Saint Anton's well shall be my drink,
   Since my true-love has forsaken me.

Martinmas wind, when wilt thou blaw,
   And shake the green leaves off the tree?
O gentle death, when wilt thou come?
   For of my life I am weary.

'Tis not the frost that freezes fell,
   Nor blawing snaw's inclemency;
'Tis not sic cauld that makes me cry,
   But my love's heart grown cauld to me.

When we came in by Glasgow town,
   We were a comely sight to see;
My love was cled in the black velvet,
   And I mysel in cramasie.

But had I wist, before I kiss'd,
   That love had been sae ill to win,
I'd locked my heart in a case of gold,
   And pinn'd it with a silver pin.

Oh, oh, if my young babes were born,
   And set upon the nurse's knee,
And I mysel were dead and gane!
   For a maid again I'll never be.

Anon.

The Oak and the Ash

A north-country maid up to London had strayed,
Although with her nature it did not agree;
She wept and she sighed, and she bitterly cried,
'I wish once again in the north I could be.
   Oh! the Oak, and the Ash, and the bonny Ivy tree,
   They flourish at home in my own country.'

'While sadly I roam I regret my dear home,
Where lads and young lasses are making the hay;
The merry bells ring, and the birds sweetly sing,
And maidens and meadows are pleasant and gay.
   Oh! the Oak, and the Ash, etc.

'No doubt did I please, I could marry with ease;
Where maidens are fair many lovers will come;
But he whom I wed must be north-country bred,
And carry me back to my north country home.
   Oh! the oak, and the Ash, etc.

Anon.

Early One Morning

Early one morning, just as the sun was rising,
   I heard a maid sing in the valley below:
'Oh, don't deceive me; Oh, never leave me!
   How could you use a poor maiden so?

'Oh, gay is the garland, and fresh are the roses,
   I've culled from the garden to bind on thy brow.
Oh, don't deceive me; Oh, never leave me!
   How could you use a poor maiden so?

'Remember the vows that you made to your Mary,
   Remember the bow'r where you vow'd to be true.
Oh, don't deceive me; Oh, never leave me!
   How could you use a poor maiden so?'

Thus sang the poor maiden, her sorrows bewailing,
   Thus sang the poor maid in the valley below:
'Oh, don't deceive me; Oh, never leave me!
   How could you use a poor maiden so?'

Anon.

I Know Where I'm Going

I know where I'm going,
I know who's going with me,
I know who I love,
But the dear knows who I'll marry.

I'll have stockings of silk,
Shoes of fine green leather,
Combs to buckle my hair
And a ring for every finger.

Feather beds are soft,
Painted rooms are bonny;
But I'd leave them all
To go with my love Johnny.

Some say he's dark,
I say he's bonny,
He's the flower of them all
My handsome, coaxing Johnny.

I know where I'm going,
I know who's going with me,
I know who I love,
But the dear knows who I'll marry.

Anon., Irish

The Keel Row

As I cam' doon the Sandgate, the Sandgate, the Sandgate,
As I cam' doon the Sandgate, I heard a lassie sing! } (twice)
  'O weel may the keel row, the keel row, the keel row,
  O weel may the keel row the ship my laddie's in.'

My love he wears a bonnet, a bonnet, a bonnet,
A snawy rose upon it, a dimple in his chin. } (twice)
  O weel may the keel row, etc.

And soon I heard her lover, her lover, her lover,
Had landed from the Rover, and joined her in this strain. } (twice)
  O weel may the keel row, etc.

Anon.

Scarborough Fair

Are you going to Scarborough Fair?
  Parsley, sage, rosemary, and thyme;
Remember me to one who lives there,
  For once she was a true love of mine.

Tell her to make me a cambric shirt,
  Parsley, sage, rosemary, and thyme;
Without any seam or needlework,
  For once she was a true love of mine.

Tell her to wash it in yonder well,
  Parsley, sage, rosemary, and thyme;
Where never spring water or rain ever fell,
  For once she was a true love of mine.

Tell her to dry it on yonder thorn,
  Parsley, sage, rosemary, and thyme;
Which never bore blossom since Adam was born,
  For once she was a true love of mine.

Now he has asked me questions three,
  Parsley, sage, rosemary, and thyme;
I hope he will answer as many for me,
  For once he was a true love of mine.

Tell him to find me an acre of land,
  Parsley, sage, rosemary, and thyme;
Betwixt the salt water and the sea-sand,
  For once he was a true love of mine.

Tell him to plough it with a ram's horn,
  Parsley, sage, rosemary, and thyme;
And sow it all over with one pepper corn,
  For once he was a true love of mine.

Tell him to reap it with a sickle of leather,
  Parsley, sage, rosemary, and thyme,
And bind it up with a peacock's feather,
  For once he was a true love of mine.

When he has done and finished his work,
  Parsley, sage, rosemary, and thyme;
O tell him to come and he'll have his shirt,
  For once he was a true love of mine.   Anon.

The Lass of Richmond Hill

On Richmond Hill there lives a lass,
  More bright than May-day morn,
Whose charms all other maids surpass,
  A rose without a thorn.
    This lass so neat, with smiles so sweet,
      Has won my right good will,
    I'd crowns resign to call thee mine,
      Sweet Lass of Richmond Hill.

Ye zephyrs gay that fan the air,
  And wanton thro' the grove,
O whisper to my charming fair,
  I die for her I love.
    This lass so neat, etc.

How happy will the Shepherd be
  Who calls this Nymph his own.
O may her choice be fixed on me,
  Mine's fixed on her alone.
    This lass so neat, etc.

W. Upton

Sally in our Alley

Of all the girls that are so smart
  There's none like pretty Sally,
She is the darling of my heart
  And lives in our alley.
There is no lady in the land
  Is half so sweet as Sally,
She is the darling of my heart,
  And lives in our alley.

Of all the days that's in the week
  I dearly love but one day,
And that's the day that comes betwixt
  A Saturday and Monday;
For then I'm drest, in all my best,
  To walk abroad with Sally;
She is the darling of my heart,
  And lives in our alley.

My master carries me to church,
  And often I am blamed,
Because I leave him in the lurch
  As soon as text is named.
I leave the church in sermon-time,
  And slink away to Sally;
She is the darling of my heart,
  And lives in our alley.

My master and the neighbours all
  Make game of me and Sally;
And (but for her) I'd better be
  A slave and row a galley:
But when my seven long years are out
  O! then I'll marry Sally!
And then we'll wed and then we'll bed,
  But not in our alley.

Henry Carey c. 1687–1743

Where'er You Walk

Where'er you walk, cool gales shall fan the glade;
Trees, where you sit, shall crowd into a shade;
Where'er you tread, the blushing flowers shall rise,
And all things flourish where you turn your eyes.

Alexander Pope 1688–1744

O, My Luve is like a Red, Red Rose

O, my luve is like a red, red rose,
   That's newly sprung in June:
O, my luve is like the melodie
   That's sweetly played in tune.

As fair art thou, my bonnie lass,
   So deep in luve am I;
And I will luve thee still, my dear,
   Till a' the seas gang dry.

Till a' the seas gang dry, my dear,
   And the rocks melt wi' the sun:
And I will luve thee still, my dear,
   While the sands o' life shall run.

And fare thee weel, my only luve,
   And fare thee weel a while!
And I will come again, my luve,
   Tho' it were ten thousand mile!

Robert Burns 1759–1796

Sweet Afton

Flow gently, sweet Afton! among thy green braes,
Flow gently, I'll sing thee a song in thy praise;
My Mary's asleep by thy murmuring stream,
Flow gently, sweet Afton, disturb not her dream.

Thou stock-dove whose echo resounds thro' the glen,
Ye wild whistling blackbirds in yon thorny den,
Thou green crested lapwing, thy screaming forbear,
I charge you, disturb not my slumbering Fair.

How lofty, sweet Afton, thy neighbouring hills,
Far marked with the courses of clear, winding rills;
There daily I wander as noon rises high,
My flocks and my Mary's sweet cot in my eye.

How pleasant thy banks and green valleys below,
Where, wild in the woodlands, the primroses blow;
There oft, as mild ev'ning weeps over the lea,
The sweet-scented birk shades my Mary and me.

Thy crystal stream, Afton, how lovely it glides,
And winds by the cot where my Mary resides;
How wanton thy waters her snowy feet lave,
As, gathering sweet flowerets, she stems thy clear wave.

Flow gently, sweet Afton, among thy green braes,
Flow gently, sweet river, the theme of my lays;
My Mary's asleep by thy murmuring stream,
Flow gently, sweet Afton, disturb not her dream.

Robert Burns 1759–1796

93

O Whistle, and I'll Come to Ye

O whistle, and I'll come to ye, my lad,
O whistle, and I'll come to ye, my lad;
Tho' father, and mother, and a' should gae mad,
   Thy Jeanie will venture wi' ye, my lad.

But warily tent, when ye come to court me,
And come nae unless the back-yett be a-jee;
Syne up the back-style and let naebody see,
   And come as ye were na comin to me –
   And come as ye were na comin to me. –
     O whistle, etc.

At kirk, or at market whene'er ye meet me,
Gang by me as tho' that ye car'd nae a flie;
But steal me a blink o' your bonie black e'e,
   Yet look as ye were na lookin at me –
   Yet look as ye were na lookin at me. –
     O whistle, etc.

Ay vow and protest that ye care na for me,
And whyles ye may lightly my beauty a wee;
But court nae anither, tho' jokin ye be,
   For fear that she wyle your fancy frae me –
   For fear that she wyle your fancy frae me. –
     O whistle, etc.

Tent	take care;	*Syne*	then;
backyett	back gate;	*wyle*	charm.

Robert Burns 1759–1796

Green Grow the Rashes, O

Green grow the rashes O,
    Green grow the rashes O;
The sweetest hours that e'er I spend,
    Are spent amang the lasses O!

There's nought but care on ev'ry han',
    In ev'ry hour that passes O;
What signifies the life o' man,
    An' 'twere na for the lasses O.

The warly race may riches chase,
    An' riches still may fly them O;
An' tho' at last they catch them fast,
    Their hearts can ne'er enjoy them O.

But gie me a canny hour at e'en,
    My arms about my dearie O;
An' warly cares, an' warly men,
    May a' gae tapsalteerie O!

For you sae douce, ye sneer at this,
    Ye're nought but senseless asses O:
The wisest man the warl' saw,
    He dearly lov'd the lasses O.

Auld nature swears, the lovely dears
    Her noblest work she classes O;
Her prentice han' she tried on man,
    An' then she made the lasses O.

Auld Lang Syne

Should auld acquaintance be forgot,
    And never brought to min'?
Should auld acquaintance be forgot,
    And auld lang syne?
        For auld lang syne, my dear.
          For auld lang syne,
        We'll tak a cup o' kindness yet,
        For auld lang syne.

We twa hae run about the braes,
    And pu'd the gowans fine;
But we've wander'd mony a weary foot
    Sin' auld lang syne.
        For auld lang syne, etc.

We twa hae paidled i' the burn,
    From morning sun till dine;
But seas between us braid hae roar'd
    Sin' auld lang syne.
        For auld lang syne, etc.

And there's a hand, my trusty fiere,
    And gie 's a hand o' thine;
And we'll tak a right guid-willie waught,
    For auld lang syne.
        For auld lang syne, etc.

And surely ye'll be your pint-stowp,
    And surely I'll be mine;
And we'll tak a cup o' kindness yet
    For auld lang syne.
        For auld lang syne, etc.

Robert Burns 1759–1796

Ae Fond Kiss

Ae fond kiss, and then we sever;
Ae fareweel, and then for ever!
Deep in heart-wrung tears I'll pledge thee,
Warring sighs and groans I'll wage thee. –

Who shall say that Fortune grieves him,
While the star of hope she leaves him:
Me, nae cheerful twinkle lights me;
Dark despair around benights me. –

I'll ne'er blame my partial fancy,
Naething could resist my Nancy:
But to see her, was to love her;
Love but her, and love for ever. –

Had we never lov'd sae kindly,
Had we never lov'd sae blindly!
Never met – or never parted,
We had ne'er been broken-hearted. –

Fare-thee-weel, thou first and fairest!
Fare-thee-weel, thou best and dearest!
Thine be ilka joy and treasure,
Peace, Enjoyment, Love and Pleasure! –

Ae fond kiss, and then we sever!
Ae fareweel, Alas, for ever!
Deep in heart-wrung tears I'll pledge thee,
Warring sighs and groans I'll wage thee. –

The Banks o' Doon

Ye banks and braes o' bonnie Doon,
    How can ye bloom sae fresh and fair?
How can ye chant, ye little birds,
    And I sae weary fu' o' care?
Thou'lt break my heart, thou warbling bird,
    That wantons thro' the flowering thorn:
Thou minds me o' departed joys,
    Departed never to return.

Aft hae I rov'd by bonnie Doon,
    To see the rose and woodbine twine;
And ilka bird sang o' its love,
    And fondly sae did I o' mine.
Wi' lightsome heart I pu'd a rose,
    Fu' sweet upon its thorny tree;
And my fause lover stole my rose,
    But ah! he left the thorn wi' me.

John Anderson my Jo

John Anderson my Jo, John,
    When we were first acquent;
Your locks were like the raven,
    Your bony brow was brent;
But now your brow is beld, John,
    Your locks are like the snaw;
But blessings on your frosty pow,
    John Anderson my Jo.

John Anderson my Jo, John,
    We clamb the hill thegither;
And mony a canty day, John,
    We've had wi' ane anither:
Now we maun totter down, John,
    But hand in hand we'll go;
And sleep thegither at the foot,
    John Anderson my Jo.

pow head   *canty* jolly

Robert Burns 1759–1796

Believe me, if all those Endearing Young Charms

Believe me, if all those endearing young charms,
　　Which I gaze on so fondly to-day,
Were to change by to-morrow, and fleet in my arms,
　　Like fairy-gifts, fading away!
Thou wouldst still be ador'd, as this moment thou art,
　　Let thy loveliness fade as it will,
And, around the dear ruin, each wish of my heart
　　Would entwine itself verdantly still!

It is not, while beauty and youth are thine own,
　　And thy cheeks unprofan'd by a tear,
That the fervour and faith of a soul can be known,
　　To which time will but make thee more dear!
No, the heart that has truly lov'd, never forgets,
　　But as truly loves on to the close,
As the sun-flower turns on her god, when he sets,
　　The same look which she turn'd when he rose!

Thomas Moore 1779–1852

Comin' thro' the Rye

Gin a body meet a body,
　　Comin' thro' the rye,
Gin a body greet a body
　　Need a body cry?
　　　Ilka lassie has her laddie
　　　　Ne'er a ane hae I;
　　　But a' the lads they smile on me
　　　　When comin' thro' the rye.

Gin a body meet a body,
　　Comin' frae the well,
Gin a body kiss a body
　　Need a body tell?
　　　Ilka lassie, etc.

Gin a body meet a body,
　　Comin' frae the toun,
Gin a body kiss a body
　　Need a body gloom?
　　　Ilka lassie, etc.

Amang the train there is a swain
　　I dearly lo'e mysel': –
But whaur his hame, or what his name,
　　I dinna care to tell.
　　　Ilka lassie, etc.

Anon., collected by Burns

So, We'll Go no more A-Roving

So, we'll go no more a-roving
  So late into the night,
Though the heart be still as loving,
  And the moon be still as bright.

For the sword outwears its sheath,
  And the soul wears out the breast,
And the heart must pause to breathe,
  And love itself have rest.

Though the night was made for loving,
  And the day returns too soon,
Yet we'll go no more a-roving
  By the light of the moon.

George Gordon, Lord Byron 1788–1824

She is Far from the Land

She is far from the land where her young hero sleeps,
  And lovers are round her, sighing;
But coldly she turns from their gaze, and weeps,
  For her heart in his grave is lying!

She sings the wild song of her dear native plains,
  Every note which he lov'd awaking –
Ah! little they think, who delight in her strains,
  How the heart of the Minstrel is breaking!

He had liv'd for his love, for his country he died,
  They were all that to life had entwin'd him, –
Nor soon shall the tears of his country be dried,
  Nor long will his love stay behind him.

Oh! make her a grave, where the sun-beams rest,
  When they promise a glorious morrow;
They'll shine o'er her sleep, like a smile from the West,
  From her own lov'd Island of sorrow!

Thomas Moore 1779–1852

The Ash Grove

Down yonder green valley where streamlets meander,
  When twilight is fading, I pensively rove;
Or at the bright noontide, in solitude wander
  Amid the dark shades of the lonely Ash Grove.
'Twas there, while the blackbird was cheerfully singing,
  I first met that dear one – the joy of my heart! –
Around us for gladness the bluebells were ringing;
  Ah! then little thought I how soon we should part.

Still glows the bright sunshine o'er valley and mountain,
  Still warbles the blackbird its note from the tree;
Still trembles the moonbeam on streamlet and fountain,
  But what are the beauties of nature to me?
With sorrow, deep sorrow, my bosom is laden,
  All day I go mourning in search of my love;
Ye echoes! oh tell me, where is the sweet maiden?
  'She sleeps 'neath the green turf down by the Ash Grove.'

Anon., Traditional Welsh

Loch Lomond

By yon bonnie banks and by yon bonnie braes,
Where the sun shines bright on Loch Lomond,
Where I and my true love were ever wont to gae,
On the bonnie, bonnie banks of Loch Lomond.
    Oh you'll take the high road, an' I'll tak the low road,
    An' I'll be in Scotland afore ye;
    But I and my true love will never meet again
    On the bonnie, bonnie banks of Loch Lomond.

'Twas there that we pairted in yon shady glen,
On the steep, steep side o' Ben Lomond,
Where purple-hued the Hieland hills we viewed,
And the moon comin' out in the gloaming.
    Oh you'll take the high road, etc.

The wee birdies sing, and the wild flowers sing,
An' in sunshine the waters are sleepin',
But the broken heart it kens nae second spring,
Tho' the waefu' may cease from their greetin'.
    Oh you'll take the high road, etc.

Anon., Traditional Scottish

Cockles and Mussels

In Dublin's fair city, where girls are so pretty,
I first set my eyes on sweet Molly Malone,
As she wheeled her wheelbarrow through streets broad and narrow,
Crying, Cockles and mussels! alive, alive oh!
   Alive, alive, oh! alive, alive, oh!
   Crying, Cockles and mussels, alive, alive oh!

She was a fishmonger, but sure 'twas no wonder,
For so were her father and mother before;
And they each wheeled their barrow through streets broad and narrow,
Crying, Cockles and mussels, alive, alive oh!
   Alive, alive, oh! etc.

She died of a fever, and no one could save her,
And that was the end of sweet Molly Malone;
Her ghost wheels her barrow through streets broad and narrow,
Crying, Cockles and mussels, alive, alive oh!
   Alive, alive, oh! etc.

Anon.

Annie Laurie

Maxwellton braes are bonnie,
    Where early fa's the dew,
And it's there that Annie Laurie
    Gi'ed me her promise true –
Gi'ed me her promise true,
    Which ne'er forgot will be;
And for bonnie Annie Laurie
    I'd lay me down and dee.

Her brow is like the snaw-drift,
    Her neck is like the swan,
Her face it is the fairest
    That e'er the sun shone on;
That e'er the sun shone on,
    And dark blue is her e'e;
And for bonnie Annie Laurie
    I'd lay me down and dee.

Like dew on the gowan lying,
    Is the fa' o' her fairy feet;
And like winds in summer sighing,
    Her voice is low and sweet.
Her voice is low and sweet,
    And she's a' the world to me;
And for bonnie Annie Laurie
    I'd lay me down and dee.

Anon.

O No, John!

On yonder hill there stands a creature,
    Who she is I do not know.
I'll go and court her for her beauty;
    She must answer Yes or No.
O No John! No John! No John! No!

My father was a Spanish captain –
    Went to sea a month ago.
First he kissed me, then he left me –
    Bid me always answer No.
O No John! No John! No John! No!

O Madam in your face is beauty,
    On your lips red roses grow.
Will you take me for your lover?
    Madam, answer Yes or No.
O No John! No John! No John! No!

O Madam, I will give you jewels;
    I will make you rich and free;
I will give you silken dresses.
    Madam, will you marry me?
O No John! No John! No John! No!

O Madam, since you are so cruel,
    And that you do scorn me so,
If I may not be your lover,
    Madam, will you let me go?
O No John! No John! No John! No!

Then I will stay with you for ever,
    If you will not be unkind.
Madam, I have vowed to love you;
    Would you have me change my mind?
O No John! No John! No John! No!

O hark! I hear the church bells ringing:
    Will you come and be my wife?
Or, dear Madam, have you settled
    To live single all your life?
O No John! No John! No John! No!

Anon., Traditional Somerset

The Foggy, Foggy Dew

When I was a bachelor I lived all alone
   And I worked at the weaver's trade,
And the only, only thing that I ever did wrong
   Was to woo a fair young maid.

I wooed her in the winter time,
   And in the summer too,
And the only, only thing that I ever did wrong
   Was to keep her from the foggy, foggy dew.

One night she came to my bedside
   When I was fast asleep,
She flung her arms around my neck
   And she began to weep.

She wept, she cried, she damn near died,
   She said, What shall I do?
So I rolled her into bed and I covered up her head,
   Just to keep her from the foggy, foggy dew.

O I am a bachelor, I live with my son
   And we work at the weaver's trade,
And every single time that I look into his eyes
   He reminds me of that fair young maid.

He reminds me of the winter time
   And of the summer too,
And the many, many times I held her in my arms
   Just to keep her from the foggy, foggy dew.

Anon.

Clementine

In a cavern, in a canyon,
   Excavating for a mine,
Dwelt a miner, forty-niner,
   And his daughter Clementine.
Oh my darling, oh my darling,
Oh my darling Clementine!
Thou art lost and gone for ever,
Dreadful sorry, Clementine.

Light she was and like a fairy,
   And her shoes were number nine;
Herring-boxes, without topses,
   Sandals were for Clementine.
     Oh my darling, etc.

Drove the ducklings to the water
   Ev'ry morning, just at nine;
Hit her foot against a splinter,
   Fell into the foaming brine.
     Oh my darling, etc.

Saw her lips above the water
   Blowing bubbles mighty fine;
But alas! I was no swimmer,
   So I lost my Clementine.
     Oh my darling, etc.

In a corner of the churchyard,
   Where the myrtle boughs entwine,
Grow the roses in their posies,
   Fertilised by Clementine.
     Oh my darling, etc.

Then the miner, forty-niner,
   Soon began to peak and pine,
Thought he 'oughter jine' his daughter.
   Now he's with his Clementine.
     Oh my darling, etc.

In my dreams she still doth haunt me,
   Robed in garments soaked in brine;
Though in life I used to hug her,
   Now she's dead I'll draw the line.
     Oh my darling, etc.

How I missed her, how I missed her,
   How I missed my Clementine!
But I kissed her little sister,
   And forgot my Clementine.
     Oh my darling, etc.

Percy Montrose

Sweet and Low

from 'The Princess'

Sweet and low, sweet and low,
   Wind of the western sea,
Low, low, breathe and blow,
   Wind of the western sea!
Over the rolling waters go,
Come from the dying moon, and blow,
   Blow him again to me;
While my little one, while my pretty one, sleeps.

Sleep and rest, sleep and rest,
   Father will come to thee soon;
Rest, rest, on mother's breast,
   Father will come to thee soon;
Father will come to his babe in the nest,
Silver sails all out of the west
   Under the silver moon:
Sleep, my little one, sleep, my pretty one, sleep.

Alfred, Lord Tennyson 1809–1892

Come into the Garden, Maud

Come into the garden, Maud,
For the black bat, Night, has flown;
Come into the garden, Maud,
I am here at the gate alone.
I am here at the gate alone;
And the woodbine spices are wafted abroad,
And the musk of the rose is blown,
For a breeze of morning moves,
And the planet of love is on high,
Beginning to faint in the light that she loves,
On a bed of daffodil sky,
To faint in the light of the sun she loves,
To faint in his light and to die.
Come! Come!

Come into the garden, Maud,
For the black bat, Night, has flown,
Come into the garden, Maud,
I am here at the gate alone.

Queen rose of the rosebud garden of girls,
Come hither, the dances are done;
In gloss of satin and glimmer of pearls,
Queen lily, and rose in one.
Shine out, little head running over with curls,
To the flowers, and be their sun.
Shine out! Shine out! and be their sun.

Come into the garden, Maud,
For the black bat, Night, has flown;
Come into the garden, Maud,
She is coming, my own, my sweet,
Were it ever so airy a tread,
My heart would hear her and beat,
Were it earth in an earthy bed.

Come, my own, my sweet,
Come, my own, my sweet,
Maud, Maud, come,
I am here at the gate alone.

Alfred, Lord Tennyson 1809–1892

All Through the Night

Sleep, my love, and peace attend thee,
    All through the night;
Guardian angels God will lend thee,
    All through the night;
Soft the drowsy hours are creeping,
Hill and dale in slumber steeping,
Love alone his watch is keeping –
    All through the night.

Though I roam a minstrel lonely,
    All through the night,
My true harp shall praise thee only,
    All through the night;
Love's young dream, alas, is over,
Yet my strains of love shall hover
Near the presence of my lover,
    All through the night.

Hark! a solemn bell is ringing,
    Clear through the night;
Thou, my love, art heavenward winging,
    Home through the night;
Earthly dust from off thee shaken,
Soul immortal thou shalt waken,
With thy last dim journey taken
    Home through the night.

Harold Boulton

Jeanie with the Light Brown Hair

I dream of Jeanie, with the light brown hair
Borne like a zephyr on the summer air;
I see her tripping where the bright streams play,
Happy as the daisies that dance on her way.
Many were the wild notes her merry voice would pour,
Many were the blithe birds that warbled them o'er:
I dream of Jeanie, with the light brown hair
Floating like a zephyr on the soft, summer air.

I sigh for Jeanie, but her light form strayed
Far from the fond hearts round her native glade,
Her smiles have vanished and her sweet songs flown,
Flitting like the dreams that have cheered us and gone.
Now the nodding wild flow'rs may wither on the shore,
While her gentle fingers will cull them no more;
I sigh for Jeanie with the light brown hair,
Floating like a zephyr on the soft, summer air.

Beautiful Dreamer

Beautiful dreamer, wake unto me,
Starlight and dewdrops are waiting for thee.
Sounds of the rude world heard in the day,
Lull'd by the moonlight,.have all pass'd away.

Beautiful dreamer, queen of my song,
List while I woo thee with soft melody.
Gone are the cares of life's busy throng.
Beautiful dreamer, awake unto me.

Beautiful dreamer, out on the sea,
Mermaids are chanting the wild lorelie.
Over the streamlet vapours are borne,
Waiting to fade at the bright coming morn.

Beautiful dreamer, beam on my heart,
E'en as the morn on the streamlet and sea.
Then will all clouds of sorrow depart.
Beautiful dreamer, awake unto me,
Beautiful dreamer, awake unto me.

Stephen Foster 1826–1864

108

Take a Pair of Sparkling Eyes

from *The Gondoliers*

Take a pair of sparkling eyes,
   Hidden, ever and anon,
     In a merciful eclipse –
Do not heed their mild surprise –
   Having passed the Rubicon.
     Take a pair of rosy lips;
Take a figure trimly planned –
   Such as admiration whets
     (Be particular in this);
Take a tender little hand,
   Fringed with dainty fingerettes,
     Press it – in parenthesis; –
Take all these, you lucky man –
Take and keep them, if you can!

Take a pretty little cot –
   Quite a miniature affair –
     Hung about with trellised vine,
Furnish it upon the spot
   With the treasures rich and rare
     I've endeavoured to define.
Live to love and love to live –
   You will ripen at your ease,
     Growing on the sunny side –
Fate has nothing more to give.
   You're a dainty man to please
     If you are not satisfied.
Take all these, you lucky man –
Take and keep them, if you can!

W.S. Gilbert 1836–1911

Bredon Hill

In summertime on Bredon
  The bells they sound so clear;
Round both the shires they ring them
  In steeples far and near,
  A happy noise to hear.

Here of a Sunday morning
  My love and I would lie,
And see the coloured counties,
  And hear the larks so high
  About us in the sky.

The bells would ring to call her
  In valleys miles away:
'Come all to church, good people;
  Good people, come and pray.'
  But here my love would stay.

And I would turn and answer
  Among the springing thyme,
'Oh, peal upon our wedding,
  And we will hear the chime,
  And come to church in time.'

But when the snows at Christmas
  On Bredon top were strown,
My love rose up so early
  And stole out unbeknown
  And went to church alone.

They tolled the one bell only,
  Groom there was none to see,
The mourners followed after,
  And so to church went she,
  And would not wait for me.

The bells they sound on Bredon,
  And still the steeples hum.
'Come all to church, good people, –'
  Oh, noisy bells, be dumb;
  I hear you, I will come.

A.E. Housman 1859–1936

In the Gloaming

In the gloaming oh! my darling when the lights are dim and low
And the quiet shadows falling softly come and softly go,
When the winds are sobbing faintly with a gentle unknown woe
Will you think of me and love me, as you did once long ago?

In the gloaming oh! my darling think not bitterly of me,
Tho' I passed away in silence, left you lonely, set you free,
For my heart was crush'd with longing, what had been could never be.

It was best to leave you thus dear, best for you and best for me.
It was best to leave you thus,
Best for you and best for me.

Meta Orred 1874

Love's Old Sweet Song

Once in the dear dead days beyond recall,
When on the world the mists began to fall,
Out of the dreams that rose in happy throng
Low to our hearts Love sung an old sweet song;
And in the dusk where fell the firelight gleam,
Softly it wove itself into our dream.
   Just a song at twilight, when the lights are low,
   And the flick'ring shadows softly come and go,
   Tho' the heart be weary, sad the day and long,
   Still to us at twilight comes Love's old song,
   Comes Love's old sweet song.

Even today we hear Love's song of yore,
Deep in our hearts it dwells for ever more.
Footsteps may falter, weary grow the way,
Still we can hear it at the close of day,
So till the end, when life's dim shadows fall,
Love will be found the sweetest song of all.
   Just a song at twilight, etc.

C. Clifford Bingham 1882

Daisy Bell

There is a flower within my heart, Daisy, Daisy!
Planted one day by a glancing dart,
Planted by Daisy Bell!
Whether she loves me or loves me not,
Sometimes it's hard to tell;
Yet I am longing to share the lot
Of beautiful Daisy Bell!
   Daisy, Daisy,
   Give me your answer, do!
   I'm half crazy,
   All for the love of you!
   It won't be a stylish marriage,
   I can't afford the carriage,
   But you'll look sweet upon the seat
   Of a bicycle built for two!

We will go tandem as man and wife, Daisy, Daisy!
Peddling away down the road of life,
I and my Daisy Bell!
When the road's dark we can both despise
P'liceman and 'lamps' as well.
There are 'bright lights' in the dazzling eyes
Of beautiful Daisy Bell!
   Daisy, Daisy, etc.

I will stand by you in 'wheel' or woe, Daisy, Daisy!
You'll be the bell(e) which I'll ring, you know!
Sweet little Daisy Bell!
You'll take the 'lead' in each 'trip' we take,
Then if I don't do well,
I will permit you to take the 'break',
My beautiful Daisy Bell!
   Daisy, Daisy, etc.

Written and composed in 1892 by Harry Dacre 1860–1922
Sung by Katie Lawrence

My Old Dutch

I've got a pal,
A reg'lar out-an'-outer.
She's a dear good old gal,
I'll tell yer all about 'er;
It's many years since fust we met,
'Er 'air was then as black as jet,
It's whiter now, but she don't fret,
Not my old gal.
   We've been together now for forty year,
   An' it don't seem a day too much,
   There ain't a lady livin' in the land,
   As I'd swop for my dear old Dutch, } *(twice)*

I call 'er Sal,
'Er proper name is Sairer,
An' yer may find a gal
As you'd consider fairer.
She ain't a angel – she can start
A-jawin' till it makes yer smart,
She's just a *woman*, bless 'er 'eart,
Is my old gal!
   We've been together now, etc.

Sweet fine old gal,
For worlds I wouldn't lose 'er,
She's a dear good old gal,
An' that's what made me choose 'er.
She's stuck to me through thick and thin,
When luck was out, when luck was in,
Ah! wot a wife to me she's been,
An' wot a *pal*!
   We've been together now, etc.

I see yer Sal –
Yer pretty ribbons sportin'!
Many years now, old gal,
Since them young days of courtin'!
I ain't a coward, still I trust
When we've to part, as part we must,
That Death may come and take me fust,
To wait . . . my pal!
   We've been together now, etc.

Written and sung in 1892 by Albert Chevalier 1861–1923

The Lily of Laguna

It's de same old tale of a palpatating niggar ev'ry time, ev'ry time;
It's de same old trouble of a coon
Dat wants to be married very soon;
It's de same old heart dat is longing for its lady ev'ry time, yes, ev'ry time.
But not de same gal, not de same gal,
She is ma Lily, ma Lily, ma Lily gal!

She goes ev'ry sundown, yes, ev'ry sundown callin' in de cattle up de mountain;
I go 'kase she wants me, yes, 'kase she wants me help her do de callin' and
    de countin'.
She plays her music to call de lone lambs dat roam above,
But I'm de black sheep and I'm waitin'
For de signal of ma little lady love.
    She's ma lady love, she is ma dove, ma baby love.
    She's no gal for sittin' down to dream,
    She's de only queen Laguna knows;
    I know she likes me,
    I know she likes me
    Bekase she says so;
    She is de Lily of Laguna,
    She is ma Lily and ma Rose.

When I first met Lil it was down in old Laguna at de dance, oder night;
So she says, 'Say, a'm curious for to know
When ye leave here de way yer goin' to go,
'Kase a wants to see who de lady is dat claims ye all way home, way home
    tonight.'
I says, 'I've no gal, never had one,'
And den ma Lily, ma Lily, ma Lily gal!
She says, 'Kern't believe ye, I kern't believe ye, else I'd like to have ye
    shapperoon me;
Dad says he'll escortch me, says he'll escortch me,
But it's mighty easy for to lose him.'
Since then each sundown I wander down here and roam around
Until I know my lady wants me,
Till I hear de music ob de signal sound.
    She's ma lady love, etc.

Written and composed by Leslie Stuart, 1898
Sung by Eugene Stratton

Kashmiri Song

Pale hands I loved beside the Shalimar,
Where are you now? Who lies beneath your spell?
Whom do you lead on Rapture's roadway, far,
Before you agonise them in farewell?
Pale hands I loved beside the Shalimar,
Where are you now? Where are you now?

Pale hands, pink tipped, like Lotus buds that float
On those cool waters where we used to dwell,
I would have rather felt you round my throat
Crushing out life, than waving me farewell!
Pale hands I loved beside the Shalimar,
Where are you now? Where are you now?

'Laurence Hope' (b. Adela Florence Cory) 1865–1904

I'll Sing thee Songs of Araby

I'll sing thee songs of Araby,
    And tales of fair Kashmir,
Wild tales to cheat thee of a sigh,
    Or charm thee to a tear,
And dreams of delight shall on thee break,
    And rainbow visions rise,
And all my soul shall strive to wake
    Sweet wonder in thine eyes,
And all my soul shall strive to wake
    Sweet wonder in thine eyes.

Through those twin lakes, when wonder wakes,
    My raptured song shall sink,
And as the diver dives for pearls,
    Bring tears, bright tears to their brink,
And dreams of delight shall on thee break,
    And rainbow visions rise,
And all my soul shall strive to wake
    Sweet wonder in thine eyes,
And all my soul shall strive to wake
    Sweet wonder in thine eyes.

W.G. Wills 1887

Frankie and Johnny

Frankie and Johnny were lovers.
Oh my Gawd how they did love!
They swore to be true to each other,
As true as the stars above.
He was her man but he done her wrong.

Frankie and Johnny went walking
Johnny in a brand new suit.
Frankie went walking with Johnny,
Said: 'O Gawd don't my Johnny look cute.'
He was her man but he done her wrong.

Frankie went down to Memphis,
Went on the morning train,
Paid a hundred dollars,
Bought Johnny a watch and chain.
He was her man but he done her wrong.

Frankie lived in a crib-house,
Crib-house with only two doors,
Gave her money to Johnny,
He spent it on those parlour whores.
He was her man but he done her wrong.

Frankie went down to the hock-shop,
Went for a bucket of beer,
Said: 'O Mr Bartender,
Has my loving Johnny been here?
He is my man but he's doing me wrong.'

'I don't want to make you no trouble,
I don't want to tell you no lie,
But I saw Johnny an hour ago
With a girl name Nelly Bly.
He is your man but he's doing you wrong.'

Frankie went down to the hotel.
She didn't go there for fun,
'Cause underneath her kimona
She toted a 44 gun.
He was her man but he done her wrong.

Frankie went down to the hotel.
She rang the front-door bell,
Said: 'Stand back all you chippies
Or I'll blow you all to hell.
I want my man for he's doing me wrong.'

Frankie looked in through the key-hole
And there before her eye
She saw her Johnny on the sofa
A-loving up Nelly Bly.
He was her man; he was doing her wrong.

Frankie threw back her kimona,
Took out her big 44,
Root-a-toot-toot, three times she shoot
Right through that hard-ware door.
He was her man but was doing her wrong.

Johnny grabbed up his Stetson,
Said: 'O my Gawd Frankie don't shoot.'
But Frankie pulled hard on the trigger
And the gun went root-a-toot-toot.
She shot her man who was doing her wrong.

'Roll me over easy,
Roll me over slow,
Roll me over on my right side
'Cause my left sides hurts me so.
I was her man but I done her wrong.'

Johnny was a gambler,
He gambled for the gain;
The very last words he ever said
Were – 'High-low Jack and the game.'
He was her man but he done her wrong.

'Bring out your rubber-tired buggy,
Bring out your rubber-tired hack;
I'll take my Johnny to the graveyard
But I won't bring him back.
He was my man but he done me wrong.

Lock me in that dungeon,
Lock me in that cell,
Lock me where the north-east wind
Blows from the corner of Hell.
I shot my man 'cause he done me wrong.'

Frankie went down to the Madame,
She went down on her knees.
'Forgive me Mrs Halcombe,
Forgive me if you please
For shooting my man 'cause he done me wrong.'

'Forgive you Frankie darling,
Forgive you I never can,
Forgive you Frankie darling
For shooting your only man,
For he was your man though he done you wrong.'

It was not murder in the first degree,
It was not murder in the third.
A woman simply shot her man
As a hunter drops a bird.
She shot her man 'cause he done her wrong.

Frankie said to the Sheriff
'What do you think they'll do?'
The Sheriff said to Frankie
'It's the electric chair for you.
You shot your man 'cause he done you wrong.'

Frankie sat in the jail-house,
Had no electric fan,
Told her little sister:
'Don't you marry no sporting man.
I had a man but he done me wrong.'

Frankie heard a rumbling,
Away down in the ground;
Maybe it was little Johnny,
Where she had shot him down.
He was her man but he done her wrong.

Once more I saw Frankie,
She was sitting in the chair
Waiting for to go and meet her God
With the sweat dripping out of her hair.
He was her man but he done her wrong.

This story has no moral,
This story has no end,
This story only goes to show
That there ain't no good in men.
He was her man but he done her wrong.

Anon.

117

St Louis Blues

I hate to see that evening sun go down;
Yes, I hate to see that evening sun go down;
Seems like my baby done left this here town.

Feeling tomorrow like I feel today,
If I'm feeling tomorrow like I feel today,
I'm gonna pack my bag and make my get-away,
   Saint Louis woman
   With her diamond rings
   Pulls that man around
   By her apron-strings;
   If it wasn't for powder
   And her store-bought hair
   That man I love
   He wouldn't go nowhere, nowhere.

Got the Saint Louis blues, just as blue as I can be,
My man's got a heart like a rock cast down deep in the sea,
Or else he wouldn't go so far from me.

I love my man like a schoolboy loves his pie;
Like a Kentucky colonel loves his mint and rye;
Gonna love that man until the day he die.

Written and composed in 1914 by W.C. Handy 1873–1958

Silver Threads among the Gold

Darling, I am growing old,
Silver threads among the gold
Shine upon my brow today,
Life is fading fast away.
But my darling, you will be, will be
Always young and fair to me,
Yes, my darling, you will be
Always young and fair to me.
   Darling, I am growing old,
   Silver threads among the gold
   Shine upon my brow today;
   Life is fading fast away.

When your hair is silver white
And your cheeks no longer bright
With the roses of the May,
I will kiss your lips and say
'Oh, my darling, mine alone, alone,
You have never older grown;
Yes, my darling, mine alone,
You have never older grown!'
   Darling, etc.

Love can never more grow old,
Locks may lose their brown and gold;
Cheeks may fade and hollow grow,
But the hearts that love will know
Never, never winter's frost and chill,
Summer warmth is in them still.
Never winter's frost and chill,
Summer warmth is in them still.
   Darling, etc.

Eben E. Rexford 1848–1916

Because

Because you come to me with naught save love
And hold my hand, and lift mine eyes above,
A wider world of hope and joy I see,
Because you come to me.

Because you speak to me in accents sweet,
I find the roses waking round my feet,
And I am led through tears and joy to thee,
Because you speak to me.

Because God made thee mine I'll cherish thee,
Through light and darkness, through all time to be,
And pray His love may make our love divine,
Because God made thee mine.

Written and composed by Guy d'Hardelot
English words by Edward Teschemacher, 1902

The English Rose

Dan Cupid hath a garden
Where women are the flow'rs,
And lovers' laughs and lovers' tears
The sunshine and the show'rs.
And oh! the sweetest blossom
That in the garden grows,
The fairest Queen it is, I ween,
The perfect English rose,
The fairest Queen it is, I ween,
The perfect, the perfect English rose.

Let others make a garden
Of ev'ry flow'r that blows!
But I will wait till I may pluck
My dainty English rose.
In perfume, grace and beauty,
The rose doth stand apart,
God grant that I, before I die,
May wear one on my heart!
God grant that I, before I die,
May wear one, may wear one on my heart,
May wear one on my heart,
May wear one on my heart.

Written by Basil Hood for Sir Edward German's
Merrie England 1902

121

Nellie Dean

By the old mill stream I'm dreaming, Nellie Dean,
Dreaming of your bright eyes gleaming, Nellie Dean,
As they used to fondly glow,
When we sat there long ago,
List'ning to the waters flow, Nellie Dean.
I can hear the robins singing, Nellie Dean,
Sweetest recollections bringing, Nellie Dean,
And they seem to sing of you
With your tender eyes of blue,
For I know they miss you too, Nellie Dean.
   There's an old mill by the stream, Nellie Dean,
   Where we used to sit and dream, Nellie Dean,
   And the waters as they flow
   Seem to murmur sweet and low,
   You're my heart's desire,
   I love you, Nellie Dean.

I recall the day we parted, Nellie Dean,
How you trembled, broken hearted, Nellie Dean,
And you pinned a rose of red
On my coat of blue and said
That a soldier boy you'd wed, Nellie Dean.
All the world seems sad and lonely, Nellie Dean,
For I love you and you only, Nellie Dean,
And I wonder if on high
You still love me, if you sigh
For the happy days gone by, Nellie Dean.
   There's an old mill, etc.

Harry Armstrong 1879–1951

Macushla

Macushla! Macushla! your sweet voice is calling,
Calling me softly again and again.
Macushla! Macushla! I hear its dear pleading,
My blue-eyed Macushla, I hear it in vain.

Macushla! Macushla! your white arms are reaching,
I feel their enfolding caressing me still.
Fling them out from the darkness, my lost love, Macushla,
Let them find me and bind me again if they will.

Macushla! Macushla! your red lips are saying
That death is a dream, and love is for aye.
Then awaken, Macushla, awake from your dreaming,
My blue-eyed Macushla, awaken to stay.

Written and composed in 1910 by Josephine V. Rowe
and Dermot MacMurrough

The Rose of Tralee

The pale moon was rising above the green mountain,
The sun was declining beneath the blue sea,
When I stray'd with my love to the pure crystal fountain
That stands in the beautiful vale of Tralee.
She was lovely and fair as the rose of the summer,
Yet 'twas not her beauty alone that won me.
Oh no! 'twas the truth in her eye ever dawning
That made me love Mary, the Rose of Tralee!

The cool shades of evening their mantle were spreading,
And Mary all smiling was list'ning to me,
The moon thro' the valley her pale rays was shedding
When I won the heart of the Rose of Tralee.
Though lovely and fair as the rose of the summer,
Yet 'twas not her beauty alone that won me.
Oh no! 'twas the truth in her eye ever dawning
That made me love Mary, the Rose of Tralee!

C. Mordaunt Spencer, 1912

123

Danny Boy

Oh, Danny Boy, the pipes, the pipes are calling
From glen to glen, and down the mountain side.
The summer's gone and all the roses falling,
It's you, it's you must go and I must bide.
But come ye back when summer's in the meadow,
Or when the valley's hushed and white with snow,
It's I'll be here in sunshine or in shadow,
Oh, Danny Boy, oh, Danny Boy, I love you so!

But when ye come, and all the flowers are dying,
If I am dead, as dead I well may be,
Ye'll come and find the place where I am lying,
And kneel and say an Ave there for me.
And I shall hear, though soft you tread above me,
And all my grave will warmer, sweeter be,
For you will bend and tell me that you love me,
And I shall sleep in peace until you come to me!

Fred E. Weatherly 1848–1929

Roses of Picardy

She is watching by the poplars,
Colinette with the sea-blue eyes,
She is watching and longing and waiting
Where the long white roadway lies.
And a song stirs in the silence,
As the wind in the boughs above.
She listens and starts and trembles,
'Tis the first little song of love: –
  'Roses are shining in Picardy,
  In the hush of the silver dew,
  Roses are flow'ring in Picardy,
  But there's never a rose like you!
  And the roses will die with the summer time,
  And our roads may be far apart,
  But there's one rose that dies not in Picardy!
  'Tis the rose that I keep in my heart!'

And the years fly on for ever,
Till the shadows veil their skies,
But he loves to hold her little hands,
And look in her sea-blue eyes.
And she sees the road by the poplars,
Where they met in the bygone years,
For the first little song of the roses
Is the last little song she hears.
  Roses are shining, etc.

Fred E. Weatherly 1848–1929

There's a Long, Long Trail

Nights are growing very lonely,
Days are very long;
I'm a-growing weary
Only listening for your song.
Old remembrances are thronging
Thro' my memory,
Thronging till it seems
The world is full of dreams
Just to call you back to me.
  There's a long, long trail a-winding
  Into the land of my dreams,
  Where the nightingales are singing
  And a white moon beams:
  There's a long, long night of waiting
  Until my dreams all come true;
  Till the day when I'll be going down
  That long, long trail with you.

All night long I hear you calling,
Calling sweet and low;
Seem to hear your footsteps falling
Ev'ry where I go.
Tho' the road between us stretches
Many a weary mile,
Somehow I forget
That you're not with me yet,
When I think I see you smile.
  There's a long, long trail, etc.

Written in 1913 by Stoddard King 1889–1933

If You Were the Only Girl in the World

Chorus
If you were the only girl in the world,
And I were the only boy,
Nothing else would matter in the world today,
We could go on loving in the same old way.
A Garden of Eden just made for two,
With nothing to mar our joy;
I would say such wonderful things to you,
There would be such wonderful things to do,
If you were the only girl in the world,
And I were the only boy.

Clifford Grey 1887–1941

I'll Walk Beside You

I'll walk beside you through the world today,
While dreams and songs and flowers bless your way,
I'll look into your eyes and hold your hand,
I'll walk beside you through the golden land.

I'll walk beside you through the world tonight,
Beneath the starry skies ablaze with light,
And in your heart love's tender words I'll hide,
I'll walk beside you through the eventide.

I'll walk beside you through the passing years,
Through days of cloud and sunshine, joy and tears;
And when the great call comes, the sunset gleams,
I'll walk beside you to the land of dreams.

Edward Lockton, 1936

A Nightingale Sang in Berkeley Square

That certain night, the night we met,
There was magic abroad in the air.
There were angels dining at the Ritz,
And a nightingale sang in Berkeley Square.

I may be right, I may be wrong,
But I'm perfectly willing to swear,
That when you turned and smiled at me,
A nightingale sang in Berkeley Square.

The moon that lingered over London Town,
Poor puzzled moon, he wore a frown,
How could he know we two were so in love
The whole darned world seemed upside down.

The streets of Town were paved with stars,
It was such a romantic affair,
And as we kissed and said goodnight
A nightingale sang in Berkeley Square.

How strange it was, how sweet and strange,
There was never a dream to compare
With that hazy, crazy night we met,
When a nightingale sang in Berkeley Square.

This heart of mine beat loud and fast,
Like a merry-go-round in a fair,
For we were dancing cheek to cheek,
And a nightingale sang in Berkeley Square.

When dawn came stealing up, all gold and blue,
To interrupt our rendezvous,
I still remember how you smiled and said,
'Was that a dream, or was it true?'

Our homeward step was just as light
As the tapdancing feet of Astaire,
And like an echo far away,
A nightingale sang in Berkeley Square.

I know 'cause I was there,
That night in Berkeley Square.

Written and composed in 1940
by Manning Sherwin

I'll Be Seeing You

I'll be seeing you
In all the old familiar places
That my heart and mind embraces all day through.
In that small café,
The park across the way,
The children's carousel,
The chestnut trees, the wishing well.
I'll be seeing you
In ev'ry lovely summer's day,
In ev'rything that's light and gay,
I'll always think of you that way.
I'll find you in the morning sun
And when the night is new,
I'll be looking at the moon,
But I'll be seeing you.

Irving Kahl, 1938

Lilli Marlene

Underneath the lantern by the barrack gate,
Darling, I remember the way you used to wait;
'Twas there that you whispered tenderly,
That you lov'd me,
You'd always be
My Lilli of the lamplight,
My own Lilli Marlene.

Time would come for roll-call, time for us to part.
Darling, I'd caress you and press you to my heart;
And there 'neath that far off lantern light,
I'd hold you tight,
We'd kiss goodnight;
My Lilli of the lamplight,
My own Lilli Marlene.

Orders came for sailing somewhere over there,
All confined to barracks was more than I could bear;
I knew you were waiting in the street,
I heard your feet,
But could not meet
My Lilli of the lamplight,
My own Lilli Marlene.

Resting in a billet just behind the line,
Even tho' we're parted your lips are close to mine;
You wait where the lantern softly gleams,
Your sweet face seems
To haunt my dreams,
My Lilli of the lamplight,
My own Lilli Marlene.

Hans Leip, c. 1944

LIFE
&
LAUGHTER

She was poor, but she was honest

She was one of the early birds

and I wuz one of the worms

Daddy wouldn't buy me a bow wow

Green Grow the Rushes O has lived on as a song for many years after most of its religious symbolism has become obscure; in fact there is a peculiar satisfaction in singing about the nine bright shiners, the six proud walkers and the rushes themselves without knowing what they stand for.* The sense of ritual is reinforced by the repetitive progression from one to twelve. Marxist and philosophical versions ('Eight for the 8th Route Army' ... 'Two, two for opposites/Interpenetrating O') and no doubt others were once current. The repetitions that are so enjoyable in the singing may look cumbrous on the page, but as in one or two other cases we satisfied ourselves that any shortened text would be a distortion and troublesome to follow.

Like many other nursery rhymes, 'Oranges and Lemons' also has ritual connections, with in this case the singers or players passing one by one through an arch of joined hands and a 'victim' pinioned at the end. One theory of origin looks back to the days of public executions, when criminals were taken to the scaffold through the streets to the ringing of church bells – the errant wives of Henry VIII are favourites. As so often, the song has successfully outlived the historical occasion of its beginnings. Whatever these may have been it is hard not to see them as much older than the 1740s, when the words were first recorded.

The collaboration of W.S. Gilbert and Arthur Sullivan provides another uniqueness of British song. Sullivan (b. 1842) was the most gifted British composer of his day. He wrote much orchestral music and a great deal for the Church (including 'Onward, Christian Soldiers'), but he is best remembered for his part in the Savoy operas of the period 1875–1890. Here, for the first and last time in English, a poet of tremendous comic and rhythmic invention met a composer who really understood the material he was setting and made it his business to display it to the best advantage. This perhaps helps to explain how entertainments that were so thoroughly the products of their era should continue to appeal in a totally different state of society.

Some of our remarks about love-songs apply to many of the pieces in this section, which also endorse what we said at the beginning about the British character as generally reflected in this book. They show how the grandparents and remoter ancestors of the present generation thought and felt about quite a large part of life, including what they aspired to or judged admirable ('Sea-Fever', 'Leaning') as well as what they might have known from personal experience ('She was one of the Early Birds', 'Don't Dilly-Dally on the Way'). Only a hasty or incurious historian of the nation could ignore such abundant and varied material.

*But the curious might like to know that, according to Geoffrey Grigson and others, those references that are not self-evident can be interpreted as follows:
One: one God, one faith, one truth, one baptism. Two: the New and Old Testaments, also Christ and John the Baptist. Three: the Trinity. Five: the five senses of man. Six: the days of the working week. (Perhaps originally 'workers'.) Seven: the planets as known in medieval times: Sun, Moon, Mercury, Venus, Mars, Jupiter, Saturn. Eight: the eight survivors of the Flood. Nine: the nine orders of angels.
It has been suggested that the rushes and their green stand for the world of Nature.

Green Grow the Rushes O

I'll sing you one O.
  Green grow the rushes O.
What is your one O?
  One is one and all alone
  And ever more shall be so.

I'll sing you two O.
  Green grow the rushes O.
What are your two O?
  Two, two, the lily-white boys,
  Clothed all in green O.
  One is one and all alone
  And ever more shall be so.

I'll sing you three O.
  Green grow the rushes O.
What is your three O?
  Three, three the rivals,
  Two, two, the lily-white boys,
  Clothed all in green O.
  One is one and all alone
  And ever more shall be so.

I'll sing you four O.
  Green grow the rushes O.
What is your four O?
  Four for the Gospel makers,
  Three, three the rivals,
  Two, two, the lily-white boys,
  Clothed all in green O,
  One is one and all alone
  And ever more shall be so.

I'll sing you five O.
  Green grow the rushes O.
What is your five O?
  Five for the symbol at your door,
  Four for the Gospel makers,
  Three, three the rivals,
  Two, two, the lily-white boys,
  Clothed all in green O,
  One is one and all alone
  And ever more shall be so.

I'll sing you six O.
  Green grow the rushes O.
What is your six O?
  Six for the six proud walkers,
  Five for the symbol at your door,
  Four for the Gospel makers,
  Three, three the rivals,
  Two, two, the lily-white boys,
  Clothed all in green O,
  One is one and all alone
  And ever more shall be so.

I'll sing you seven O.
  Green grow the rushes O.
What is your seven O?
  Seven for the seven stars in the sky,
  Six for the six proud walkers,
  Five for the symbol at your door,
  Four for the Gospel makers,
  Three, three the rivals,
  Two, two, the lily-white boys,
  Clothed all in green O,
  One is one and all alone
  And ever more shall be so.

I'll sing you eight O.
  Green grow the rushes O.
What is your eight O?
  Eight for the eight bold rangers,
  Seven for the seven stars in the sky,
  Six for the six proud walkers,
  Five for the symbol at your door,
  Four for the Gospel makers,
  Three, three the rivals,
  Two, two, the lily-white boys,
  Clothed all in green O,
  One is one and all alone
  And ever more shall be so.

continued overleaf

I'll sing you nine O.
   Green grow the rushes O.
What is your nine O?
   Nine for the nine bright shiners,
   Eight for the eight bold rangers,
   Seven for the seven stars in the sky,
   Six for the six proud walkers,
   Five for the symbol at your door,
   Four for the Gospel makers,
   Three, three the rivals,
   Two, two, the lily-white boys,
   Clothed all in green O,
   One is one and all alone
   And ever more shall be so.

I'll sing you ten O.
   Green grow the rushes O.
What is your ten O?
   Ten for the ten commandments,
   Nine for the nine bright shiners,
   Eight for the eight bold rangers,
   Seven for the seven stars in the sky,
   Six for the six proud walkers,
   Five for the symbol at your door,
   Four for the Gospel makers,
   Three, three the rivals,
   Two, two, the lily-white boys,
   Clothed all in green O,
   One for one and all alone
   And ever more shall be so.

I'll sing you eleven O.
   Green grow the rushes O.
What is your eleven O?
   Eleven for the eleven who went to heaven,
   Ten for the ten commandments,
   Nine for the nine bright shiners,
   Eight for the eight bold rangers,
   Seven for the seven stars in the sky,
   Six for the six proud walkers,
   Five for the symbol at your door,
   Four for the Gospel makers,
   Three, three the rivals,
   Two, two, the lily-white boys,
   Clothed all in green O,
   One is one and all alone,
   And ever more shall be so.

I'll sing you twelve O.
   Green grow the rushes O.
What is your twelve O?
   Twelve for the twelve apostles,
   Eleven for the eleven who went to heaven,
   Ten for the ten commandments,
   Nine for the nine bright shiners,
   Eight for the eight bold rangers,
   Seven for the seven stars in the sky,
   Six for the six proud walkers,
   Five for the symbol at your door,
   Four for the Gospel makers,
   Three, three the rivals,
   Two, two, the lily-white boys,
   Clothed all in green O,
   One is one and all alone
   And ever more shall be so.

Anon.

The Bonnie Earl of Moray

Ye Highlands and ye Lawlands,
   Oh! where hae ye been?
They hae slain the Earl of Moray,
   And hae laid him on the green.

Now wae be to thee, Huntly,
   And wherefore did you sae?
I bade you bring him wi' you,
   But forbade you him to slay.

He was a braw gallant,
   And he rid at the ring;
And the bonnie Earl of Moray,
   Oh! he might hae been a king.

He was a braw gallant,
   And he play'd at the ba';
And the bonnie Earl of Moray
   Was the flower amang them a'.

He was a braw gallant,
   And he play'd at the glove;
And the bonnie Earl of Moray,
   Oh! he was the Queen's luve.

Oh! lang will his lady,
   Look owre the castle Doune,
Ere she see the Earl of Moray
   Come sounding thro' the toun.

Anon.

Blow, Blow, thou Winter Wind

from *As You Like It*

Blow, blow, thou winter wind,
Thou art not so unkind
 As man's ingratitude;
Thy tooth is not so keen,
Because thou art not seen,
 Although thy breath be rude.
Heigh-ho! sing, heigh-ho! unto the green holly:
Most friendship is feigning, most loving mere folly.
  Then heigh-ho! the holly!
  This life is most jolly.

Freeze, freeze, thou bitter sky,
That dost not bite so nigh
 As benefits forgot:
Though thou the waters warp,
Thy sting is not so sharp
 As friend remembered not.
Heigh-ho! sing, heigh-ho! unto the green holly:
Most friendship is feigning, most loving mere folly.
  Then heigh-ho! the holly!
  This life is most jolly.

William Shakespeare 1564–1616

Here's a Health unto His Majesty

Here's a health unto his Majesty,
With a fal lal la la la la la!
Confusion to his enemies,
With a fal lal la la la la la!
And he that will not drink his health,
I wish him neither wit nor wealth,
Nor yet a rope to hang himself,
With a fal lal la . . .

All Cavaliers will please combine,
With a fal lal la la la la la!
To drink this loyal toast of mine,
With a fal lal la la la la la!
If anyone should answer 'No,'
I only wish that he may go,
With Roundhead rogues to Jericho
With a fal lal la . . .

Oranges and Lemons

Oranges and lemons,
Say the bells of St Clement's.

You owe me five farthings,
Say the bells of St Martin's.

When will you pay me?
Say the bells of Old Bailey.

When I grow rich,
Say the bells of Shoreditch.

When will that be?
Say the bells of Stepney.

I'm sure I don't know,
Says the great bell at Bow.

Here comes a candle to light you to bed,
Here comes a chopper to chop off your head.   Anon.

Down among the Dead Men

Here's a health to the King, and a lasting peace,
To faction an end, to wealth increase;
Come, let's drink it while we have breath,
For there's no drinking after death.
And he that will this health deny,
Down among the dead men let him lie.

Let charming beauty's health go round,
In whom celestial joys are found;
And may confusion still pursue
The senseless woman-hating crew;
And they that woman's health deny,
Down among the dead men let them lie.

In smiling Bacchus' joys I'll roll,
Deny no pleasure to my soul;
Let Bacchus' health round briskly move,
For Bacchus is a friend to Love.
And he that will this health deny,
Down among the dead men let him lie.

May love and wine their rites maintain,
And their united pleasures reign;
While Bacchus' treasure crowns the board,
We'll sing the joys that both afford;
And they that won't with us comply,
Down among the dead men let them lie.

John Dyer 1700–1758

Come, Landlord, Fill the Flowing Bowl

Come, landlord, fill the flowing bowl
Until it doth run over,
Come, landlord, fill the flowing bowl
Until it doth run over.
   For to-night we'll merry be,
   For to-night we'll merry be,
   For to-night we'll merry be,
   To-morrow we'll be sober.

The man who drinketh small beer,
And goes to bed quite sober,
Fades as the leaves do fade,
That drop off in October.
   For to-night we'll merry be, etc.

The man who drinketh strong beer,
And goes to bed right mellow,
Lives as he ought to live,
And dies a jolly good fellow.
   For to-night we'll merry be, etc.

But he who drinks just what he likes,
And getteth half-seas over,
Will live until he die, perhaps,
And then lie down in clover.
   For to-night we'll merry be, etc.

The man who kisses a pretty girl,
And goes and tells his mother,
Ought to have his lips cut off,
And never kiss another.
   For to-night we'll merry be, etc.

Anon.

The Vicar of Bray

In good King Charles's golden days,
  When loyalty no harm meant,
A zealous High-Churchman I was,
  And so I got preferment;
To teach my flock I never missed –
  Kings are by God appointed,
And damned are those who do resist
  Or touch the Lord's annointed.
    And this is law, I will maintain,
      Until my dying day, Sir,
    That whatsoever king shall reign,
      I'll be the Vicar of Bray, Sir.

When royal James obtained the crown,
  And Popery came in fashion,
The penal laws I hooted down,
  And read the declaration:
The Church of Rome I found would fit
  Full well my constitution,
And had become a Jesuit –
  But for the Revolution.
    And this is law, etc.

When William was our king declared
  To ease the nation's grievance,
With this new wind about I steered,
  And swore to him allegiance,
Old principles I did revoke,
  Set conscience at a distance;
Passive obedience was a joke,
  A jest was non-resistance.
    And this is law, etc.

When gracious Anne became our queen,
  The Church of England's glory,
Another face of things was seen –
  And I became a Tory:
Occasional Conformists base,
  I scorned their moderation,
And thought the church in danger was
  By such prevarication.
    And this is law, etc.

When George in pudding-time came o'er,
  And moderate men look big, Sir,
I turned a cat-in-pan once more –
  And so became a Whig, Sir:
And this preferment I procured
  From our new faith's defender,
And almost every day abjured
  The Pope and the Pretender.
    And this is law, etc.

The illustrious house of Hanover,
  And the Protestant succession,
To these I do allegiance swear –
  While they can keep possession:
For in my faith and loyalty
  I never more will falter,
And George my lawful King shall be –
  Until the times do alter.
    And this is law, etc.

Anon.

140

The Lincolnshire Poacher

When I was bound apprentice, in famous Lincolnsheer,
Full well I served my master for more than seven year,
Till I took up with poaching, as you shall quickly hear.
    Oh, 'tis my delight of a shiny night, in the season of the year.

As me and my comrades were setting of a snare,
'Twas then we seed the gamekeeper – for him we did not care.
For we can wrestle and fight, my boys, and jump o'er everywhere.
    Oh, 'tis my delight of a shiny night, in the season of the year.

As me and my comrades were setting four or five,
And taking on 'em up again, we caught the hare alive;
We caught the hare alive, my boys, and through the woods did steer.
    Oh, 'tis my delight of a shiny night, in the season of the year.

I threw him on my shoulder, and then we trudged home,
We took him to a neighbour's house and sold him for a crown,
We sold him for a crown, my boys, but I did not tell you where.
    Oh, 'tis my delight of a shiny night, in the season of the year.

Bad luck to every magistrate that lives in Lincolnsheer;
Success to every poacher that wants to sell a hare;
Bad luck to every gamekeeper that will not sell his deer.
    Oh, 'tis my delight of a shiny night, in the season of the year.

Anon.

Spanish Ladies

Farewell and adieu to you, fair Spanish Ladies,
   Farewell and adieu to you, Ladies of Spain,
For we've received orders to sail for Old England,
   But we hope in a short time to see you again.
     We'll rant and we'll roar, all o'er the wild ocean,
     We'll rant and we'll roar, all o'er the wild seas,
     Until we strike soundings in the Channel of Old England,
     From Ushant to Scilly is thirty-five leagues.

We hove our ship to, with the wind at sou-west, boys,
   We hove our ship for to strike soundings clear;
Then filled the main topsail and bore right away, boys,
   And straight up the Channel our course we did steer.
     We'll rant and we'll roar, etc.

The first land we made was a point called the Dodman,
   Next Rame Head off Plymouth, Start, Portland and Wight.
We sailed then by Beachy, by Fairlee and Dung'ness,
   Then bore straight away for the South Foreland Light.
     We'll rant and we'll roar, etc.

The signal was made for the Grand Fleet to anchor,
   We clewed up our topsails, stuck out tacks and sheets,
We stood by our stoppers, we brailed in our spanker,
   And anchored ahead of the noblest of fleets.
     We'll rant and we'll roar, etc.

Then let every man here toss off a full bumper,
   Then let every man here toss off his full bowl,
For we will be jolly and drown melancholy,
   With a health to each jovial and true-hearted soul.
     We'll rant and we'll roar, etc.

Anon.

Tom Bowling

Here, a sheer hulk, lies poor Tom Bowling,
    The darling of our crew;
No more he'll hear the tempest howling,
    For Death has broached him to.
His form was of the manliest beauty,
    His heart was kind and soft,
Faithful below he did his duty,
    And now he's gone aloft.

Tom never from his word departed,
    His virtues were so rare,
His friends were many, and true hearted,
    His Poll was kind and fair:
And then he'd sing so blithe and jolly,
    Ah many's the time and oft!
But mirth is turned to melancholy,
    For Tom is gone aloft.

Yet shall poor Tom find pleasant weather,
    When he who all commands
Shall give, to call life's crew together,
    The word to pipe all hands.
Thus Death, who Kings and tars dispatches,
    In vain Tom's life has doffed,
For, though his body's under hatches,
    His soul is gone aloft.

Charles Dibdin 1745–1814

Widdicombe Fair

'Tom Pearce, Tom Pearce, lend me your grey mare,
All along, down along, out along, lea,
For I want for to go to Widdicombe Fair,
Wi' Bill Brewer, Jan Stewer, Peter Gurney,
Peter Davy, Dan'l Whiddon, Harry Hawke,
　Old Uncle Tom Cobley and all,
　Old Uncle Tom Cobley and all.'

'And when shall I see again my grey mare?'
All along, down along, out along, lea,
'By Friday soon, or Saturday noon,
Wi' Bill Brewer,' etc.

Then Friday came, and Saturday noon,
All along, down along, out along, lea,
But Tom Pearce's old mare hath not trotted home,
Wi' Bill Brewer, etc.

So Tom Pearce he got up to the top o' the hill,
All along, down along, out along, lea,
And he seed his old mare down a-making her will,
Wi' Bill Brewer, etc.

So Tom Pearce's old mare, her took sick and died,
All along, down along, out along, lea,
And Tom he sat down on a stone, and he cried
Wi' Bill Brewer, etc.

But this isn't the end o' this shocking affair,
All along, down along, out along, lea,
Nor, though they be dead, of the horrid career
Of Bill Brewer, etc.

When the wind whistles cold on the moor of a night,
All along, down along, out along, lea,
Tom Pearce's old mare doth appear, gashly white,
Wi' Bill Brewer, etc.

And all the long night be heard skirling and groans,
All along, down along, out along, lea,
From Tom Pearce's old mare in her rattling bones,
And from Bill Brewer, etc.

Anon.

144

Little Brown Jug

My wife and I liv'd all alone,
In a little log-hut we call'd our own;
She lov'd gin and I lov'd rum –
I tell you what, we'd lots of fun.
    Ha-ha-ha, you and me,
    Little brown jug, don't I love thee. } *twice*

'Tis you who make my friends my foes,
'Tis you who make me wear old clothes;
Here you are, so near my nose,
So tip her up and down she goes.
    Ha-ha-ha, etc.

When I go toiling to my farm,
I take little brown jug under my arm;
I place it under a shady tree –
Little brown jug 'tis you and me.
    Ha-ha-ha, etc.

If all the folks in Adam's race,
Were gather'd together in one place;
Then I'd prepare to shed a tear,
Before I'd part from you, my dear.
    Ha-ha-ha, etc.

If I'd a cow that gave such milk,
I'd clothe her in the finest silk;
I'd feed her on the choicest hay,
And milk her forty times a day.
    Ha-ha-ha, etc.

The rose is red, my nose is, too,
The violet's blue and so are you;
And yet I guess, before I stop,
We'd better take another drop.
    Ha-ha-ha, etc.

Anon.

145

There is a Tavern in the Town

There is a tavern in the town, in the town,
And there my dear love sits him down, sits him down,
And drinks his wine 'mid laughter free
And never, never thinks of me.
    Fare thee well, for I must leave thee,
    Do not let the parting grieve thee,
    And remember that the best of friends must part, must part.
    Adieu, kind friends, adieu, adieu, adieu, adieu,
    I can no longer stay with you, stay with you.
    I'll hang my harp on a weeping willow tree,
    And may the world go well with thee.

He left me for a damsel dark, damsel dark,
Each Friday night they used to spark, used to spark,
And now my love, once true to me,
Takes that dark damsel on his knee.
    Fare thee well, etc.

Oh! dig my grave both wide and deep, wide and deep,
Put tombstones at my head and feet, head and feet,
And on my breast carve a turtle dove
To signify I died of love.
    Fare thee well, etc.

Anon.

Bonnie Charlie's Now Awa

Bonnie Charlie's now awa,
Safely owre the friendly main;
Mony a heart will break in twa,
Should he ne'er come back again.
   Will ye no come back again?
   Will ye no come back again?
   Better lo'ed ye canna be,
   Will ye no come back again?

Ye trusted in your Hieland men,
They trusted you, dear Charlie;
They kent you hiding in the glen,
Death and exile braving.
   Will ye no, etc.

Mony a gallant sodger fought,
Mony a gallant chief did fa';
Death itself were dearly bought,
A' for Scotland's king and law.
   Will ye no, etc.

Sweet's the laverock's note and lang,
Lilting wildly up the glen;
But aye to me he sings ae sang,
'Will ye no come back again?'
   Will ye no, etc.

Carolina Oliphant, Lady Nairne 1766–1845

Charlie is my Darling

Charlie is my darling, my darling, my darling,
Charlie is my darling, the young Chevalier.

'Twas on a Monday morning,
   Right early in the year,
When Charlie came to our toun,
   The young Chevalier.
      Oh! Charlie, etc.

As he came marching up the street,
   The pipes played loud and clear,
And a' the folk came running out
   To meet the Chevalier.
      Oh! Charlie, etc.

Wi' Hieland bonnets on their heads,
   And claymores bright and clear,
They came to fight for Scotland's right,
   And the young Chevalier.
      Oh! Charlie, etc.

They've left their bonnie Hieland hills,
   Their wives and bairnies dear,
To draw the sword for Scotland's lord,
   The young Chevalier.
      Oh! Charlie, etc.

Oh, there were mony beating hearts,
   And mony a hope and fear;
And mony were the pray'rs put up
   For the young Chevalier.
      Oh! Charlie, etc.

Carolina Oliphant, Lady Nairne 1766–1845

John Peel

D'ye ken John Peel with his coat so gay,
D'ye ken John Peel at the break of day,
D'ye ken John Peel when he's far, far away,
With his hounds and his horn in the morning?
   For the sound of his horn brought me from my bed,
   And the cry of his hounds which he oft-times led,
   Peel's 'View halloo' would awaken the dead
   Or the fox from his lair in the morning.

Yes, I ken John Peel, and Ruby too,
Ranter and Ringwood, Bellman and True,
From a find to a check, from a check to a view,
From a view to a death in the morning.
   For the sound of his horn, etc.

Then here's to John Peel from my heart and soul,
Let's drink to his health, let's finish the bowl,
We'll follow John Peel thro' fair and thro' foul
If we want a good hunt in the morning.
   For the sound of his horn, etc.

D'ye ken John Peel with his coat so gay?
He lived at Troutbeck once on a day,
Now he has gone far, far, far away,
We shall ne'er hear his voice in the morning.
   For the sound of his horn, etc.

John W. Graves 1795–1886

149

The Three Huntsmen

There were three jovial Welshmen,
   As I have heard them say,
And they would go a-hunting, boys,
   Upon St David's Day.
All the day they hunted,
   And nothing could they find,
But a ship a-sailing,
   A-sailing with the wind.
     And a-hunting they did go.

One said it was a ship,
   The other he said, Nay;
The third said it was a house
   With the chimney blown away.
And all the night they hunted,
   And nothing could they find,
But the moon a-gliding,
   A-gliding with the wind.
     And a-hunting they did go.

One said it was the moon,
   The other he said, Nay;
The third said it was a cheese
   And half o't cut away.
And all the day they hunted,
   And nothing could they find,
But a hedgehog in a bramble bush,
   And that they left behind.
     And a-hunting they did go.

The first said it was a hedgehog,
   The second he said, Nay;
The third, it was a pincushion,
   The pins stuck in wrong way.
And all the night they hunted,
   And nothing could they find,
But a hare in a turnip field,
   And that they left behind.
     And a-hunting they did go.

The first said it was a hare,
   The second he said, Nay;
The third, he said it was a calf,
   And the cow had run away.
And all the day they hunted,
   And nothing could they find,
But an owl in a holly-tree
   And that they left behind.
     And a-hunting they did go.

One said it was an owl,
   The second he said, Nay;
The third said t'was an old man,
   And his beard growing grey.
Then all three jovial Welshmen
   Came riding home at last,
'For three days we have nothing killed,
   And never broke our fast!'
     And a-hunting they did go.

Anon.

Bonnie Dundee

To the Lords of Convention 'twas Claver'se who spoke,
'Ere the King's crown shall fall there are crowns to be broke;
Then each cavalier who loves honour and me,
Let him follow the bonnet of Bonnie Dundee.
   'Come fill up my cup, come fill up my can,
   Come saddle your horses, and call up your men;
   Come open the West Port, and let me gang free,
   And it's room for the bonnets of Bonnie Dundee!'

Dundee he is mounted, he rides up the street,
The bells are rung backward, the drums they are beat;
But the Provost, douce man, said, 'Just e'en let him be,
The Gude Town is weel quit o' that De'il of Dundee.'
   'Come fill up my cup,' etc.

'There are hills beyond Pentland, and lands beyond Forth,
If there's lords in the Lowlands, there's chiefs in the North;
There are wild Duniewassals, three thousand times three,
Will cry "hoigh!" for the bonnet of Bonnie Dundee.
   'Come fill up my cup,' etc.

'Away to the hills, to the caves, to the rocks –
Ere I own an usurper, I'll couch with the fox;
And tremble, false Whigs, in the midst of your glee,
You have not seen the last of my bonnet and me.
   'Come fill up my cup,' etc.

Sir Walter Scott 1771–1832

The Mermaid

'Twas in the Atlantic Ocean,
   In the equinoctial gales,
A man did tumble overboard,
   Amongst the sharks and whales;
And then his ghost ap-pear-i-ed,
   Saying, Weep no more for me,
'Cos I'm mar-ri-ed to a mer-mi-ade,
    At the bottom of the deep blue sea.
      Singing, Rule Britannia, Britannia rules the waves;
      Britons never, never, never, shall be
      Mar-ri-ed to a mer-mi-ade,
      At the bottom of the deep blue sea.

Surpris'd will be my com-ri-ades,
   And the friends I've got left on the shore
And my poor grandmother, whom, alas!
   I never shall see more,
When she hears as I've been summoned
   Away quite suddenlee,
To be mar-ri-ed to a mer-mi-ade,
    At the bottom of the deep blue sea,
      Singing, Rule Britannia, etc.

There's a brocken sixpence in my purse,
   Likewise a lock of hair,
To Sally I solicitize,
   As you will safely bear;
And you will say unto her,
   It was bare necessitee
That made me wed this here mer-mi-ade,
   At the bottom of the deep blue sea,
      Singing, Rule Britannia, etc.

'Tis true, that to refresh myself,
   No baccy now I gets,
But, then, as with respects to that,
   Myself I never frets,
For all the joys of life are
   Immaterial to me
Now I'm mar-ri-ed to a mer-mi-ade,
   At the bottom of the deep blue sea,
      Singing, Rule Britannia, etc.

When I see'd and heer'd this here drownded man,
   My limbs with terror shook,
I ax'ed him qui-es-ti-ons,
   For the words my lips forsook;
And then straightways he swoonded,
   And said no more unto me,
But dived down to his mer-mi-ade,
   At the bottom of the deep blue sea.
      Singing, Rule Britannia, etc.

Version by William Makepeace Thackeray 1811–1863

Home! Sweet Home

'Mid pleasures and Palaces though we may roam,
Be it ever so humble, there's no place like home!
A charm from the skies seems to hallow us there,
Which seek through the world, is ne'er met with elsewhere.
   Home! Home! sweet sweet Home!
   There's no place like Home!
   There's no place like Home!

An Exile from Home Splendour dazzles in vain.
Oh! give me my lowly thatch'd Cottage again!
The Birds singing gaily that came at my call
Give me them with the peace of mind dearer than all.
   Home! Home! etc.

John Howard Payne 1791–1852

The Owl and the Pussy-Cat

The Owl and the Pussy-Cat went to sea
   In a beautiful pea-green boat,
They took some honey, and plenty of money,
   Wrapped up in a five-pound note.
The Owl looked up to the stars above,
   And sang to a small guitar,
'O lovely Pussy! O Pussy, my love,
   What a beautiful Pussy you are,
       You are,
       You are!
   What a beautiful Pussy you are!'

Pussy said to the Owl, 'You elegant fowl!
   How charmingly sweet you sing!
O let us be married! too long we have tarried:
   But what shall we do for a ring?'
They sailed away, for a year and a day,
   To the land where the Bong-tree grows
And there in a wood a Piggy-wig stood
   With a ring at the end of his nose,
       His nose,
       His nose,
   With a ring at the end of his nose.

'Dear Pig, are you willing to sell for one shilling
   Your ring?' Said the Piggy, 'I will.'
So they took it away, and were married next day
   By the Turkey who lives on the hill.
They dined on mince, and slices of quince,
   Which they ate with a runcible spoon;
And hand in hand, on the edge of the sand,
   They danced by the light of the moon,
       The moon,
       The moon,
   They danced by the light of the moon.

Edward Lear 1812–1888

154

The Sands of Dee

'O Mary, go and call the cattle home,
        And call the cattle home,
        And call the cattle home
    Across the sands of Dee;'
The western wind was wild and dank with foam,
    And all alone went she.

The western tide crept up along the sand,
        And o'er and o'er the sand,
        And round and round the sand,
    As far as eye could see.
The rolling mist came down and hid the land:
    And never home came she.

'Oh! is it weed, or fish, or floating hair –
        A tress of golden hair,
        A drownèd maiden's hair
    Above the nets at sea?
Was never salmon yet that shone so fair
    Among the stakes on Dee.'

They rowed her in across the rolling foam,
        The cruel crawling foam,
        The cruel hungry foam,
    To her grave beside the sea:
But still the boatman hear her call the cattle home
    Across the sands of Dee.

Charles Kingsley 1819–1875

Camptown Races

De Camptown ladies sing dis song,
   Doodah! doodah!
De Camptown race-track five miles long,
   Oh! doodah day!
I come down dah wid my hat caved in,
   Doodah! doodah!
I go back home wid a pocket full of tin,
   Oh! doodah day!
   Gwine to run all night!
   Gwine to run all day!
   I'll bet my money on de bob-tail nag,
   Somebody bet on de bay.

De long-tail filly and de big black hoss,
   Doodah! doodah!
Dey fly de track and dey both cut across,
   Oh! doodah day!
De blind hoss stick'n in a big mud hole,
   Doodah! doodah!
Can't touch de bottom wid a ten-foot pole,
   Oh! doodah day!
   Gwine to run, etc.

Old muley cow come on to de track,
   Doodah! doodah!
De bob-tail fling her ober his back,
   Oh! doodah day!
Den fly along like a rail-road car,
   Doodah! doodah!
And run a race wid a shootin' star,
   Oh! doodah day!
   Gwine to run, etc.

See dem flyin' on a ten-mile heat,
   Doodah! doodah!
Round de race-track, den repeat,
   Oh! doodah day!
I win my money on de bob-tail nag,
   Doodah! doodah!
I keep my money in an old tow bag.
   Oh! doodah day!
   Gwine to run, etc.

The Old Folks at Home

'Way down upon de Swanee Ribber,
   Far, far away,
Dere's where my heart is turning ebber:
   Dere's where de old folks stay.
All up and down de whole creation
   Sadly I roam,
Still longing for de old plantation,
   And for de old folks at home.
     All de world am sad and dreary,
      Eb'rywhere I roam.
     O darkeys, how my heart grows weary
      Far from de old folks at home.

All round de little farm I wandered
   When I was young;
Den many happy days I squandered,
   Many de songs I sung.
When I was playing wid my brudder,
   Happy was I.
Oh! take me to my kind old mudder;
   Dere let me lib and die.
     All de world, etc.

One little hut among de bushes,
   One dat I love
Still sadly to my mem'ry rushes.
   No matter where I rove.
When shall I see de bees a-humming,
   All round de comb?
When shall I hear de banjo thrumming
   Down in my good old home?
     All de world, etc.

Stephen Foster 1826–1864

156

Simon the Cellarer

Old Simon the Cellarer keeps a large store
   Of Malmsey and Malvoisie,
And Cyprus, and who can say how many more!
   For a chary old soul is he: (*twice*)
Of Sack and Canary he never doth fail,
And all the year round there is brewing of ale;
Yet he never aileth, he quaintly doth say,
While he keeps to his sober six flagons a day.
   But ho! ho! ho! his nose doth show
   How oft the black-jack to his lips doth go.

Dame Margery sits in her own still room,
   And a matron sage is she;
From thence oft at curfew is wafted a fume –
   She says it is Rosemarie! (*twice*)
But there's a small cupboard behind the back stair,
And the maids say they often see Margery there;–
Now Margery says that she grows very old,
And must take a something to keep out the cold.
   But ho! ho! ho! old Simon doth know
   Where many a flask of his best doth go!

Old Simon reclines in his high-back'd chair,
   And talks about taking a wife;
And Margery often is heard to declare
   She ought to be settled in life: (*twice*)
But Margery has (so the maids say) a tongue,
And she's not very handsome, and not very young;
So somehow it ends with a shake of the head,
And Simon, he brews him a tankard instead.
   While ho! ho! ho! he will chuckle and crow,
   'What! marry old Margery? Oh! no! no!'

W.H. Bellamy ?1800–1866

The Tarpaulin Jacket

A tall stalwart lancer lay dying,
And as on his death-bed he lay, he lay,
To his friends who around him were sighing,
These last dying words he did say:–
    Wrap me up in my tarpaulin jacket, jacket,
    And say a poor buffer lies low, lies low,
    And six stalwart lancers shall carry me, carry me,
    With steps solemn, mournful, and slow.

O had I the wings of a little dove,
Far, far away would I fly, I'd fly,
Straight for the arms of my true love;
And there would I lay me and die.
    Wrap me up, etc.

Then get you two little white tombstones,
Put them one at my head and my toe, my toe,
And get you a penknife and scratch there:
'Here lies a poor buffer below.'
    Wrap me up, etc.

And get you six brandies and sodas,
And set them all out in a row, a row,
And get you six jolly fellows,
To drink to this buffer below.
    Wrap me up, etc.

And then in the calm of the twilight,
When the soft winds are whispering low, so low,
And the darkening shadows are falling,
Sometimes think of this buffer below.
    Wrap me up, etc.

George Whyte-Melville 1821–1878

Oh, Lucky Jim

Jim and I as children played together,
Best of friends for many years were we.
I, alas! had no luck, was a Jonah,
Jim, my chum, was lucky as could be.
   Oh, lucky Jim, how I envy him! (*twice*)

Years passed by, still Jim and I were comrades.
He and I both loved the same sweet maid.
She loved Jim, and married him one evening.
Jim was lucky, I unlucky stayed.
   Oh, lucky Jim, how I envy him! (*twice*)

Years rolled on, and death took Jim away, boys,
Left his widow, and she married me.
Now we're married, oft I think of Jim, boys,
Sleeping in the churchyard peacefully.
   Oh, lucky Jim, how I envy him! (*twice*)

Anon., American.

She was Poor, but she was Honest,

She was poor, but she was honest,
    Victim of the squire's whim.
First he loved her, then he left her,
    And she lost her honest name.

Then she ran away to London,
    For to hide her grief and shame,
There she met another squire,
    And she lost her name again.

See her riding in her carriage,
    In the Park and all so gay,
All the nibs and nobby persons,
    Come to pass the time of day.

See the little old-world village,
    Where her aged parents live,
Drinking the champagne she sends them,
    But they never can forgive.

In the rich man's arms she flutters,
    Like a bird with broken wing,
First he loved her, then he left her,
    And she hasn't got a ring.

See him in the splendid mansion,
    Entertaining with the best,
While the girl that he has ruined,
    Entertains a sordid guest.

See him in the House of Commons,
    Making laws to put down crime,
While the victim of his passions
    Trails her way through mud and slime.

Standing on the bridge at midnight,
    She says: Farewell, blighted Love.
There's a scream, a splash – Good Heavens!
    What is she a-doing of?

Then they drag her from the river,
    Water from her clothes they wrung,
For they thought that she was drownded,
    But the corpse got up and sung:

It's the same the whole world over,
    It's the poor that gets the blame,
It's the rich that get the pleasure.
    Ain't it all a blooming shame?

Anon.

Eton Boating Song

Jolly boating weather
And a hay harvest breeze,
Blade on the feather,
Shade off the trees.
Swing, swing together,
With your backs between your knees,
Swing, swing together,
With your backs between your knees.

Harrow may be more clever,
Rugby may make more row,
But we'll row, row for ever,
Steady from stroke to bow.
And nothing in life shall sever
The chain that is round us now,
And nothing in life shall sever
The chain that is round us now.

Others will fill our places,
Dress'd in the old light blue,
We'll recollect our races,
We'll to the flag be true,
And youth will be still in our faces
When we cheer for an Eton crew,
And youth will be still in our faces
When we cheer for an Eton crew.

Twenty years hence this weather
May tempt us from office stools,
We may be slow on the feather,
And seem to the boys old fools,
But we'll still swing together
And swear by the best of schools,
But we'll still swing together
And swear by the best of schools.

William Johnson 1823–1892

Polly Perkins of Paddington Green

I'm a broken-hearted Milkman, in grief I'm array'd,
Through keeping of the company of a young servant maid;
Who lived on board wages, the house to keep clean,
In a gentleman's fam'ly near Paddington Green.
Oh! she was as beautiful as a Butterfly, and as proud as a Queen,
Was pretty little Polly Perkins of Paddington Green.

Her eyes were as black as the pips of a pear,
No rose in the garden with her cheeks could compare,
Her hair hung in ringerlets so beautiful and long.
I thought that she lov'd me, but found I was wrong.
Oh! she was, etc.

When I'd rattle in a morning, and cry 'milk below'
At the sound of my milk cans her face she would show,
With a smile upon her countenance and a laugh in her eye,
If I thought she'd have lov'd me, I'd have laid down to die,
For she was, etc.

When I asked her to marry me, she said, 'Oh what stuff!'
And told me to 'drop it for she'd had quite enough
Of my nonsense.' At the same time I'd been very kind,
But to marry a milkman she didn't feel inclin'd.
Oh! she was, etc.

'Oh the man that has me must have silver and gold,
A chariot to ride in, and be handsome and bold:
His hair must be curly as any watchspring,
And his whiskers as big as a brush for clothing.'
Oh! she was, etc.

The words that she utter'd went straight thro' my heart,
I sobbed, I sighed, and straight did depart
With a tear on my eyelid as big as a bean,
Bidding goodbye to Polly Perkins and Paddington Green.
Ah! she was, etc.

In six months she married, this hard-hearted girl,
But it was not a 'Wicount' and it was not a 'Nearl',
It was not a 'Barronite' but a shade or two 'wus'.
'Twas a bow-legg'd Conductor of a Twopenny 'Bus.
In spite of all she was, etc.

Harry Clifton, 1824–?
Published in 1863

162

Champagne Charlie

I've seen a deal of gaiety
  Throughout my noisy life,
With all my grand accomplishments
  I never could get a wife.
The thing I most excel in is
  The jolly party game,
A noise all night, in bed all day,
  And swimming in champagne.
    For Champagne Charlie is my name,
    Champagne Charlie is my game,
    Good for any game at night, my boys,
    Good for any game at night, my boys,
    For Champagne Charlie is my game,
    Good for any game at night, my boys,
    Who'll come and join me in a spree?

The way I gained my title's
  By a hobby which I've got
Of never letting others pay
  However long the shot;
Whoever drinks at my expense
  Are treated all the same,
From Dukes and Lords, to cabmen down,
  I make them drink Champagne.
    For Champagne Charlie, etc.

From Coffee and from Supper Rooms,
  From Poplar to Pall Mall,
The girls, on seeing me, exclaim
  'Oh, what a Champagne Swell!'
The notion 'tis of everyone
  If 'twere not for my name,
And causing so much to be drunk,
  They'd never make Champagne.
    For Champagne Charlie, etc.

Some epicures like Burgundy,
  Hock, Claret, and Moselle,
But Moet's vintage only
  Satisfies this Champagne swell.
What matter if to bed I go
  Dull head and muddled thick,
A bottle in the morning
  Sets me right then very quick.
    For Champagne Charlie, etc.

Perhaps you fancy what I say
  Is nothing else but chaff,
And only done, like other songs
  To merely raise a laugh.
To prove that I am not in jest,
  Each man a bottle of Cham.
I'll stand fizz round, yes that I will,
  And stand it like a lamb.

Written and sung by
George Leybourne 1842–1884
Composed in c. 1868 by Alfred Lee

The Flying Trapeze

Once I was happy but now I'm forlorn,
Like an old coat that is tatter'd and torn,
Left on this wide world to fret and to mourn,
Betray'd by a maid in her teens.
The girl that I loved she was handsome.
I tried all I knew her to please,
But I could not please her one quarter so well,
Like that man upon the Trapeze.
   He'd fly through the air with the greatest of ease,
   A daring young man on the flying Trapeze.
   His movements were graceful, all girls he could please,
   And my love he purloined away.

This young man by name was 'Signor Bona Slang',
Tall, big, and handsome as well made as Chang,
Where'er he appeared the Hall loudly rang
With ovation from all people there.
He'd smile from the bar on the people below
And one night he smiled on my love.
She winked back at him and she shouted 'Bravo!'
As he hung by his nose up above.
   He'd fly through the air, etc.

Her father and mother were both on my side
And very hard tried to make her my own bride,
Her father he sighed and her mother she cried,
To see her throw herself away.
'Twas all no avail she went there ev'ry night
And would throw him Bouquets on the stage.
Which caused him to meet her, how he ran me down
To tell you would take a whole page.
   He'd fly through the air, etc.

One night I as usual went to her dear home,
Found there her father and mother alone.
I asked for my love and soon they made known,
To my horror, that she'd run away!
She'd packed up her box and eloped in the night
With him with the greatest of ease.
From two storeys high he had lowered her down
To the ground on his flying Trapeze!
   He'd fly through the air, etc.

Some months after this I went to a Hall,
Was greatly surprised to see on the wall
A bill in red letters which did my heart gall,
That she was appearing with him.
He taught her gymnastics and dressed her in tights
To help him to live at his ease
And made her assume a masculine name
And now she goes on the Trapeze!
   She floats through the air with the greatest of ease,
   You'd think her a man on the flying Trapeze.
   She does all the work while he takes his ease,
   And that's what's become of my love.

Written and sung by George Leybourne 1842–1884
Composed in 1868 by Alfred Lee

165

A Modern Major-General

from *The Pirates of Penzance*

GENERAL.   I am the very pattern of a modern major-gineral:
I've information vegetable, animal, and mineral;
I know the kings of England, and I quote the fights historical,
From Marathon to Waterloo, in order categorical;
I'm very well acquainted, too, with matters mathematical;
I understand equations, both the simple and quadratical;
About binomial theorem I'm teeming with a lot of news –
Lot o' news – lot o' news –
With many cheerful facts about the square of the hypotenuse;
With many cheerful facts about the square of the hypotenuse!

ALL.   With many cheerful facts about the square of the hypotenuse!

GENERAL.   I'm very good at integral and differential calculus;
I know the scientific names of beings animalculous;
In short, in matters vegetable, animal, and mineral
I am the very model of a modern major-gineral!

ALL.   In short in matters vegetable, animal, and mineral
He is the very model of a modern major-gineral!

GENERAL.   I know our mythic history, King Arthur's and Sir Caradoc's;
I answer hard acrostics; I've a pretty taste for paradox –
I quote in elegiacs all the crimes of Heliogabalus;
In conics I can floor peculiarities parabolous;
I can tell undoubted Raphaels from Gerard Dows and Zoffanies;
I know the croaking chorus from the *Frogs* of Aristophanes;
Then I can hum a fugue of which I've heard the music's din
    afore –
Din afore? din afore, din afore? –
And whistle all the airs from that infernal nonsense, *Pinafore*,
And whistle all the airs from that infernal nonsense, *Pinafore*.

ALL.   And whistle all the airs from that infernal nonsense, *Pinafore*.

GENERAL.   Then I can write a washing-bill in Babylonic cuneiform,
                    And tell you every detail of Caractacus's uniform.
                    In short, in matters vegetable, animal, and mineral,
                    I am the very pattern of a modern major-gineral!

ALL.   In short, in matters vegetable, animal, and mineral
                    He is the very pattern of a modern major-gineral!

GENERAL.   In fact, when I know what is meant by 'mamelon' and 'ravelin' –
                    When I can tell at sight a chassepot rifle from a javelin –
                    When such affairs as sorties and surprises I'm more wary at,
                    And when I know precisely what is meant by 'commissariat' –
                    When I have learnt what progress has been made in modern
                            gunnery –
                    When I know more of tactics than a novice in a nunnery, –
                    In short, when I've a smattering of elemental strategy –
                    Strategy! strategy! –
                    You'll say a better major-gineral has never *sat* agee.

ALL.   We'll say a better major-gineral has never sat agee.

GENERAL.   For my military knowledge, though I'm plucky and adventury,
                    Has only been brought down to the beginning of the century;
                    But still, in learning vegetable, animal, and mineral
                    I am the very model of a modern major-gineral.

ALL.   But still in learning vegetable, animal, and mineral
                    He is the very model of a modern major-gineral.

W.S. Gilbert 1836–1911

When Britain Really Ruled the Waves

from *Iolanthe*

When Britain really ruled the waves –
　(In good Queen Bess's time)
The House of Peers made no pretence
To intellectual eminence,
　Or scholarship sublime;
Yet Britain won her proudest bays
In good Queen Bess's glorious days!
　　Chorus. Yes, Britain won, etc.

When Wellington thrashed Bonaparte,
　As every child can tell,
The House of Peers throughout the war,
Did nothing in particular,
　And did it very well:
Yet Britain set the world a-blaze
In good King George's glorious days!
　　Chorus. Yes, Britain set, etc.

And while the House of Peers withholds
　Its legislative hand,
And noble statesmen do not itch
To interfere with matters which
　They do not understand,
As bright will shine Great Britain's rays,
As in King George's glorious days!
　　Chorus. Yes, bright will shine, etc.

The Ruler of the Queen's Navee

from *H.M.S. Pinafore*

Sɪʀ Jᴏsᴇᴘʜ.	When I was a lad I served a term
	As office boy to an attorney's firm.
	I cleaned the windows and I swept the floor,
	And I polished up the handle of the big front door.
	I polished up that handle so carefullee
	That now I am the Ruler of the Queen's Navee!
Cʜᴏʀᴜs.	He polished, etc.

SIR JOSEPH.	As office boy I made such a mark That they gave me the post of a junior clerk. I served the writs with a smile so bland, And I copied all the letters in a big round hand – 　　I copied all the letters in a hand so free, 　　　That now I am the Ruler of the Queen's Navee!
CHORUS.	He copied, etc.
SIR JOSEPH.	In serving writs I made such a name That an articled clerk I soon became; I wore clean collars and a bran'-new suit For the pass examination at the Institute, 　　And that pass examination did so well for me, 　　　That now I am the Ruler of the Queen's Navee!
CHORUS.	And that pass examination, etc.
SIR JOSEPH.	Of legal knowledge I acquired such a grip That they took me into the partnership. And that junior partnership, I ween, Was the only ship that I ever had seen. 　　But that kind of ship so suited me, 　　　That now I am the Ruler of the Queen's Navee!
CHORUS.	But that kind, etc.
SIR JOSEPH.	I grew so rich that I was sent By a pocket borough into Parliament. I always voted at my party's call, And I never thought of thinking for myself at all. 　　I thought so little, they rewarded me 　　　By making me the Ruler of the Queen's Navee!
CHORUS.	He thought so little, etc.
SIR JOSEPH.	Now landsmen all, whoever you may be, If you want to rise to the top of the tree, If your soul isn't fettered to an office stool, Be careful to be guided by this golden rule – 　　Stick close to your desks and never go to sea, 　　　And you all may be Rulers of the Queen's Navee!
CHORUS.	Stick close, etc.

W.S. Gilbert 1836–1911

A Policeman's Lot is not a Happy One

from *The Pirates of Penzance*

SERGEANT. When a felon's not engaged in his employment –
ALL.　　His employment,
SERGEANT. Or maturing his felonious little plans –
ALL.　　Little plans,
SERGEANT. His capacity for innocent enjoyment –
ALL.　　– Cent enjoyment
SERGEANT. Is just as great as any honest man's –
ALL.　　Honest man's.
SERGEANT. Our feelings we with difficulty smother –
ALL.　　– Culty smother,
SERGEANT. When constabulary duty's to be done –
ALL.　　To be done.
SERGEANT. Ah, take one consideration with another –
ALL.　　With another,
SERGEANT. A policeman's lot is not a happy one –
ALL.　　Happy one.
　　　　When constabulary duty's to be done –
　　　　To be done –
　　　　The policeman's lot is not a happy one –
　　　　Happy one!

SERGEANT. When the enterprising burglar's not a-burgling –
ALL.　　Not a-burgling,
SERGEANT. When the cut-throat isn't occupied in crime –
ALL.　　– Pied in crime,
SERGEANT. He loves to hear the little brook a-gurgling –
ALL.　　Brook a-gurgling,
SERGEANT. And listen to the merry village chime –
ALL.　　Village chime.
SERGEANT. When the coster's finished jumping on his mother –
ALL.　　On his mother,
SERGEANT. He loves to lie a-basking in the sun –
ALL.　　In the sun.
SERGEANT. Ah, take one consideration with another –
ALL.　　With another,
SERGEANT. The policeman's lot is not a happy one –
ALL.　　Happy one!
　　　　When constabulary duty's to be done –
　　　　To be done,
　　　　The policeman's lot is not a happy one –
　　　　Happy one!

W.S. Gilbert 1836–1911

The Contemplative Sentry

from *Iolanthe*

When all night long a chap remains
    On sentry-go, to chase monotony
He exercises of his brains,
    That is, assuming that he's got any.
Though never nurtured in the lap
    Of luxury, yet I admonish you,
I am an intellectual chap,
    And think of things that would astonish you.
        I often think it's comical – Fal, lal, la!
        How Nature always does contrive – Fal, lal, la!
          That every boy and every gal
            That's born into the world alive
          Is either a little Liberal
            Or else a little Conservative!
              Fal, lal, la!

When in that House M.P.'s divide,
    If they've a brain and cerebellum, too,
They've got to leave that brain outside,
    And vote just as their leaders tell 'em to.
But then the prospect of a lot
    Of dull M.P.'s in close proximity,
All thinking for themselves, is what
    No man can face with equanimity.
        Then let's rejoice with loud Fal la – Fal lal la!
        That Nature always does contrive – Fal lal la!
          That every boy and every gal
            That's born into the world alive
          Is either a little Liberal
            Or else a little Conservative!
              Fal, lal la!

W.S. Gilbert 1836–1911

Three Little Maids

from *The Mikado*

THE THREE.	Three little maids from school are we,
	Pert as a school girl well can be,
	Filled to the brim with girlish glee,
	Three little maids from school!
YUM-YUM.	Everything is a source of fun.
PEEP-BO.	Nobody's safe, for we care for none!
PITTI-SING.	Life is a joke that's just begun!
THE THREE.	Three little maids from school!
ALL (*dancing*).	Three little maids who, all unwary,
	Come from a ladies' seminary,
	Freed from its genius tutelary –
THE THREE.	Three little maids from school!
YUM-YUM.	One little maid is a bride, Yum-Yum –
PEEP-BO.	Two little maids in attendance come –
PITTI-SING.	Three little maids is the total sum.
THE THREE.	Three little maids from school!
YUM-YUM.	From three little maids take one away –
PEEP-BO.	Two little maids remain, and they –
PITTI-SING.	Won't have to wait very long, they say –
THE THREE.	Three little maids from school!
ALL.	Three little maids who, all unwary,
	Come from a ladies' seminary,
	Freed from its genius tutelary –
THE THREE.	Three little maids from school!

W.S. Gilbert 1836–1911

Titwillow

from *The Mikado*

On a tree by a river a little tom-tit
    Sang 'Willow, titwillow, titwillow!'
And I said too him, 'Dicky-bird, why do you sit
    Singing "Willow, titwillow, titwillow"?
Is it weakness of intellect, birdie?' I cried,
'Or a rather tough worm in your little inside?'
With a shake of his poor little head he replied,
    'Oh willow, titwillow, titwillow!'

He slapped at his chest, as he sat on that bough,
    Singing 'Willow, titwillow, titwillow!'
And a cold perspiration bespangled his brow,
    Oh willow, titwillow, titwillow!
He sobbed and he sighed, and a gurgle he gave,
Then he threw himself into the billowy wave,
And an echo arose from the suicide's grave –
    'Oh willow, titwillow, titwillow!'

Now I feel just as sure as I'm sure that my name
    Isn't Willow, titwillow, titwillow,
That 'twas blighted affection that made him exclaim,
    'Oh willow, titwillow, titwillow!'
And if you remain callous and obdurate, I
Shall perish as he did, and you will know why,
Though I probably shall not exclaim as I die,
    'Oh willow, titwillow, titwillow!'

W.S. Gilbert 1836–1911

The Duke of Plaza-Toro

from *The Gondoliers*

In enterprise of martial kind,
    When there was any fighting,
He led his regiment from behind –
    He found it less exciting.
But when away his regiment ran,
    His place was at the fore, O –
        That celebrated,
        Cultivated,
        Underrated,
          Nobleman,
The Duke of Plaza-Toro!

ALL.   In the first and foremost flight, ha, ha!
You always found that knight, ha, ha!
        That celebrated,
        Cultivated,
        Underrated
          Nobleman,
The Duke of Plaza-Toro!

DUKE.   When to evade Destruction's hand
    To hide they all proceeded,
No soldier in that gallant band
    Hid half as well as he did.
He lay concealed throughout the war.
    And so preserved his gore, O!
        That unaffected,
        Undetected,
        Well-connected
          Warrior,
The Duke of Plaza-Toro!

ALL.   In every doughty deed, ha, ha!
He always took the lead, ha, ha!
        That unaffected,
        Undetected,
        Well-connected,
          Warrior,
The Duke of Plaza-Toro!

DUKE.   When told that they would all be shot
    Unless they left the service,
That hero hesitated not,
    So marvellous his nerve is.
He sent his resignation in,
    The first of all his corps, O!
        That very knowing,
        Overflowing,
        Easy-going,
          Paladin,
The Duke of Plaza-Toro!

ALL.   To men of grosser clay, ha, ha!
He always showed the way, ha, ha!
        That very knowing,
        Overflowing,
        Easy-going,
          Paladin,
The Duke of Plaza-Toro!

W.S. Gilbert 1835–1911

Linden Lea

Within the woodlands, flow'ry gladed,
By the oak trees' mossy moot,
The shining grass blades, timber shaded,
Now do quiver under foot;
And birds do whistle overhead,
And water's bubbling in its bed;
And there for me,
The apple tree
Do lean down low in Linden Lea.

When leaves, that lately were a-springing,
Now do fade within the copse,
And painted birds do hush their singing,
Up upon the timber tops;
And brown leaved fruit's a-turning red,
In cloudless sunshine overhead,
With fruit for me,
The apple tree
Do lean down low in Linden Lea.

Let other folk make money faster,
In the air of dark-roomed towns:
I don't dread a peevish master,
Though no man may heed my frowns.
I be free to go abroad,
Or take again my homeward road,
To where, for me,
The apple tree
Do lean down low in Linden Lea.

after William Barnes 1801–1886

Two Lovely Black Eyes

Strolling so happy down Bethnal Green,
This gay youth you might have seen,
Tomkins and I with his girl between,
Oh what a surprise . . . !
I praised the Conservatives frank and free,
Tomkins got angry so speedily,
All in a moment he handed to me
Two lovely black eyes.
   Two lovely black eyes!
   Oh what a surprise!
   Only for telling a man he was wrong,
   Two lovely black eyes.

Next time I argued I thought it best
To give the Conservative side a rest,
The merits of Gladstone I freely pressed,
When Oh, what a surprise!
The chap I had met was a Tory true,
Nothing the Liberals right could do,
This was my share of that argument too,
   Two lovely black eyes! etc.

The moral you've caught I can hardly doubt,
Never on politics rave and shout,
Leave it to others to fight it out,
If you would be wise.
Better, far better it is to let
Lib'rals and Tories alone, you bet,
Unless you're willing and anxious to get
   Two lovely black eyes! etc.

Charles Coborn 1852–1945

176

The Man Who Broke the Bank at Monte Carlo

I've just got here, through Paris, from the sunny southern shore;
I to Monte Carlo went, just to raise my winter's rent;
Dame Fortune smiled upon me as she'd never done before,
And I've now such lots of money, I'm a gent.
Yes, I've now such lots of money, I'm a gent.
   As I walk along the Bois Boolong
   With an independent air
   You can hear the girls declare
   'He must be a Millionaire.'
   You can hear them sigh, and wish to die,
   You can see them wink the other eye
   At the man who broke the bank at Monte Carlo.

I stay indoors till after lunch, and then my daily walk
To the great Triumphal Arch is one grand triumphal march.
Observed by each observer with the keenness of a hawk,
I'm a mass of money, linen, silk, and starch –
I'm a mass of money, linen, silk, and starch.
   As I walk along the Bois Boolong, etc.

I patronised the tables at the Monte Carlo hell
Till they hadn't got a *sou* for a Christian or a Jew;
So I quickly went to Paris for the charms of mad'moiselle,
Who's the lodestone of my heart – what can I do,
When with twenty tongues she swears that she'll be true?
   As I walk along the Bois Boolong, etc.

Written and composed in 1892 by Fred Gilbert (d. 1903)
Sung by Charles Coborn

Following in Father's Footsteps

To follow in your father's footsteps is a motto for each boy,
And following in father's footsteps is a thing I much enjoy.
My mother caught me out one evening, up the West End on the spree;
She said, 'Where are you going?' but I answered, 'Don't ask *me!*'

First Chorus:
I'm following in father's footsteps, I'm following the dear old dad.
He's just in front with a big fine gal, so I thought I'd have one as well.
I don't know where he's going, but when he gets there, I'll be glad!
I'm following in father's footsteps, yes, I'm following the dear old dad.

Pa said that to the North of England he on bus'ness had to go,
To Charing Cross he went, and there he booked, I booked first class also.
I found myself that night in Paris, to the clergyman next door
I answered when he said, 'What are you in this gay place for?'

Second Chorus:
To follow in your father's footsteps is a motto for each boy,
He's trav'ling now for his firm you see, in fancy goods it seems to me.
My mother caught me out one evening, up the West End on the spree;
She said, 'Where are you going?' but I answered, 'Don't ask *me!*'

At Margate with papa I toddled out to have a good old swim,
I didn't know the proper place to bathe, so I left it all to him.
I found myself amongst some ladies, and enjoyed it; so did pa!
Till ma yelled, 'Percy, fie for shame!' Said I, 'It's all right ma!'

Third Chorus:
To follow in your father's footsteps is a motto for each boy,
He's just out there with fair Miss Jupp to show me how to hold girls up.
I'm going to hold her next, ma, but when he drops her I'll be glad.
She said, 'Where are you going?' but I answered, 'Don't ask *me!*'

To dinner up in town last night I went, and pa went there as well,
How many 'lemonades' we had – my word! I really couldn't tell.
At two a.m. pa started off for home, like *this*, and so did I!
Folks said, 'Mind where you're going!' but I simply made reply –

Fourth Chorus:
To follow in your father's footsteps is a motto for each boy,
He's wobbling on the front, you see, and 'pon my word he's worse than me.'
My mother caught me out one evening, up the West End on the spree;
She said, 'Where are you going?' but I answered 'Don't ask *me!*'

Written in 1902 by E.W. Roger for Vesta Tilley

She was One of the Early Birds

It was at the Pantomime
Mabel and I did meet.
She was in the ballet (front row)
And I in a five shilling seat.
She was dress'd like a dickey bird –
Beautiful wings she had on.
Figure divine, wish'd she was mine.
On her I was totally gone.
    She was a dear little dickey bird,
    'Chip, chip, chip,' she went,
    Sweetly she sang to me
    Till all my money was spent.
    Then she went off song –
    We parted on fighting terms.
    She was one of the early birds,
    And I was one of the worms.

At the stage door ev'ry night
I waited with my bouquet,
Till my bird had moulted, and then
We'd drive in a hansom away.
Oyster suppers and sparkling cham –
Couldn't she go it! – What ho! –
Fivers I spent – tenners I lent,
For to her I couldn't say 'No.'
    She was a dear little dickey bird, etc.

Eel-skin coats and diamond rings
Knocked holes in my purse alone;
She would have 'em, and in the end
I got hers by pawning my own.
When at last I was fairly broke,
'Twixt us a quarrel arose –
Mabel the fair pulled out my hair,
And clawed all the skin off my nose.
    She was a dear little dickey bird, etc.

Full of love and poverty,
And armed with a carving knife,
One dark night I knelt in the mud
And asked her if she'd be my wife.
Something struck me behind the ear –
Someone said, 'Now go and get
Wife of your own – leave mine alone!'
And that was the last time we met.
    She was a dear little dickey bird, etc.

Written and composed in 1895 by T.W. Connor (d.1936)
Sung by George Beauchamp

A Bird in a Gilded Cage

The ballroom was filled with fashion's throng,
It shone with a thousand lights,
And there was a woman who passed along,
The fairest of all the sights.
A girl to her lover then softly sighed,
'There's riches at her command.'
'But she married for wealth, not for love,' he cried,
'Though she lives in a mansion grand.'
   She's only a bird in a gilded cage,
   A beautiful sight to see,
   You may think she's happy and free from care,
   She's not, though she seems to be,
   'Tis sad when you think of her wasted life,
   For youth cannot mate with age,
   And her beauty was sold,
   For an old man's gold,
   She's a bird in a gilded cage.

The beautiful woman surveyed the scene,
Her flatterers by the score;
Her gems were the purest, her gown divine,
So what could a woman want more?
But memory brings back the face of a lad,
Whose love she had turned aside,
But happiness cannot be bought with gold,
Although she's a rich man's bride.
   She's only a bird, etc.

I stood in a church-yard just at eve,
When a sunset adorned the west;
And looked at the people who'd come to grieve,
For loved ones now laid at rest.
A tall marble monument marked the grave,
Of one who'd been fashion's queen,
And I thought she is happier here at rest
Than to have people say, when seen:
   She's only a bird, etc.

Arthur J. Lamb, 1900
First sung by Florrie Forde

180

Waltzing Matilda

Once a jolly swagman camped by a billabong,
   Under the shade of a coolabah tree;
And he sang as he watched and waited till his billy boiled,
   'You'll come a-waltzing Matilda with me!'

   'Waltzing Matilda, Waltzing Matilda,
     You'll come a-waltzing Matilda with me,'
   And he sang as he watched and waited till his billy boiled,
     You'll come a-waltzing Matilda with me.'

Down came a jumbuck to drink at the billabong,
   Up jumped the swagman and grabbed him with glee;
And he sang as he shoved that jumbuck in his tucker-bag,
   'You'll come a-waltzing Matilda with me.'

   'Waltzing Matilda, Waltzing Matilda,
     You'll come a-waltzing Matilda with me,'
   And he sang as he shoved that jumbuck in his tucker-bag,
     'You'll come a-waltzing Matilda with me.'

Up rode the squatter mounted on his thoroughbred;
   Down came the troopers – one, two and three.
'Whose the jolly jumbuck you've got in your tucker-bag?
   You'll come a-waltzing Matilda with me.'

   'Waltzing Matilda, Waltzing Matilda,
     You'll come a-waltzing Matilda with me,
   Whose the jolly jumbuck you've got in your tucker-bag?
     You'll come a-waltzing Matilda with me.'

Up jumped the swagman, sprang into the billabong,
   'You'll never catch me alive,' said he.
And his ghost may be heard as you pass by that billabong
   'Who'll come a-waltzing Matilda with me?'

   'Waltzing Matilda, Waltzing Matilda,
     You'll come a-waltzing Matilda with me,'
   And his ghost may be heard as you pass by that billabong,
     'Who'll come a-waltzing Matilda with me?'

A. B. Pateson

Mandalay

By the old Moulmein Pagoda, lookin' lazy at the sea,
There's a Burma girl a-settin', and I know she thinks o' me;
For the wind is in the palm-trees, and the temple-bells they say:
'Come you back, you British soldier; come you back to Mandalay!'
    Come you back to Mandalay,
    Where the old Flotilla lay:
    Can't you 'ear their paddles chunkin' from Rangoon to Mandalay?
    On the road to Mandalay,
    Where the flyin'-fishes play,
    An' the dawn comes up like thunder outer China 'crost the Bay!

'Er petticoat was yaller an' 'er little cap was green,
An' 'er name was Supi-yaw-lat – jes' the same as Thee-baw's Queen,
An' I seed her first a-smokin' of a whackin' white cheroot,
An' a-wastin' Christian kisses on an 'eathen idol's foot:
    Bloomin' idol made o' mud –
    Wot they called the Great Gawd Budd –
    Plucky lot she cared for idols when I kissed 'er where she stud!
    On the road to Mandalay, etc.

When the mist was on the rice-fields an' the sun was droppin' slow,
She'd git 'er little banjo an' she'd sing '*Kulla-lo-lo!*'
With 'er arm upon my shoulder an' 'er cheek agin my cheek
We useter watch the steamers an' the *hathis* pilin' teak.
    Elephints a-pilin' teak
    In the sludgy, squdgy creek,
    Where the silence 'ung that 'eavy you was 'arf afraid to speak!
    On the road to Mandalay, etc.

But that's all shove be'ind me – long ago an' fur away,
An' there ain't no 'buses runnin' from the Bank to Mandalay;
An' I'm learnin' 'ere in London what the ten-year soldier tells:
'If you've 'eard the East a-callin', you won't never 'eed naught else.'
    No! you won't 'eed nothin' else
    But them spicy garlic smells,
    An' the sunshine an' the palm-trees an' the tinkly temple-bells;
    On the road to Mandalay, etc.

I am sick o' wastin' leather on these gritty pavin'-stones,
An' the blasted English drizzle wakes the fever in my bones;
Tho' I walks with fifty 'ousemaids outer Chelsea to the Strand,
An' they talks a lot o' lovin', but wot do they understand?
   Beefy face an' grubby 'and –
   Law! wot do they understand?
   I've a neater, sweeter maiden in a cleaner, greener land!
   On the road to Mandalay, etc.

Ship me somewheres east of Suez, where the best is like the worst,
Where there aren't no Ten Commandments an' a man can raise a thirst;
For the temple-bells are callin', an' it's there that I would be –
By the old Moulmein Pagoda, lookin' lazy at the sea;
   On the road to Mandalay,
   Where the old Flotilla lay,
   With our sick beneath the awnings when we went to Mandalay!
   On the road to Mandalay, etc.

Rudyard Kipling 1865–1936

Sea-Fever

I must go down to the seas again, to the lonely sea and the sky,
And all I ask is a tall ship and a star to steer her by,
And the wheel's kick and the wind's song and the white sails shaking,
And a grey mist on the sea's face and a grey dawn breaking.

I must go down to the seas again, for the call of the running tide
Is a wild call and a clear call that may not be denied;
And all I ask is a windy day with the white clouds flying,
And the flung spray and the blown spume, and the sea-gulls crying.

I must go down to the seas again, to the vagrant gypsy life,
To the gull's way and the whale's way where the wind's like a whetted knife;
And all I ask is a merry yarn from a laughing fellow-rover,
And quiet sleep and a sweet dream when the long trick's over.

John Masefield 1878–1967

Down at the old Bull and Bush

Talk about the shade of the sheltering palm,
Praise the bamboo tree with its wide spreading charm;
There's a little nook down our old Hampstead Town,
You know the place, it has won great renown.
Often with my sweetheart on a bright summer's day,
To the little pub there my footsteps will stray.
If she hesitates when she looks at the sign,
Promptly I whisper, 'Now do not decline,'
   Come, come, come and make eyes at me
   Down at the old Bull and Bush,
   Come, come, drink some port wine with me
   Down at the old Bull and Bush.
   Hear the little German band, –
   Just let me hold your hand, dear.
   Do, do, come and have a drink or two
   Down at the old Bull and Bush.

In the little parlour on a cold winter's night,
All is very cheerful, so snug and so bright;
Nell looks at me, but now not with a frown.
She would not change with the Queen and her crown.
It was there I first met the joy of my life.
She gave her troth and is now my dear wife.
Her eyes always glisten when she sees the old sign,
So all of you join in a glass of good wine,
   Come, come, come, etc.

Written in 1903 by Andrew B. Sterling, Russell Hunting
and Percy Krone
Sung by Florrie Forde

A Perfect Day

When you come to the end of a perfect day,
And you sit alone with your thought,
While the chimes ring out with a carol gay
For the joy that the day has brought,
Do you think what the end of a perfect day
Can mean to a tired heart,
When the sun goes down with a flaming ray,
And the dear friends have to part?

Well this is the end of a perfect day,
Near the end of a journey too;
But it leaves a thought that is big and strong,
With a wish that is kind and true.
For mem'ry has painted this perfect day,
With colours that never fade,
And we find at the end of a perfect day,
The soul of a friend we've made.

Carrie Jacobs-Bond, 1910

All the Nice Girls Love a Sailor

When the man-o'-war or merchant ship
Comes sailing into port,
The jolly tar with joy
Will sing out 'Land ahoy!'
With his pockets full of money
And a parrot in a cage,
He smiles at all the pretty girls
Upon the landing stage.
　　All the nice girls love a sailor,
　　All the nice girls love a tar;
　　For there's something about a sailor,
　　Well you know what sailors are:
　　Bright and breezy, free and easy,
　　He's the ladies' pride and joy;
　　Falls in love with Kate and Jane,
　　Then he's off to sea again,
　　Ship ahoy! ship ahoy!

Jack is partial to the yellow girls
Across the Eastern Seas;
With lovely almond eyes
The tar they hypnotise.
And when he goes to the Sandwich Isles
He loves the dusky belles,
Dress'd up a la Salome,
Coloured beads and oyster shells.
　　All the nice girls, etc.

He will spend his money freely
And he's gen'rous to his pals;
While Jack has got a sou,
There's half of it for you.
And it's just the same in Love or War,
He goes thro' with a smile,
And you can trust a sailor,
He's a white man all the while!
　　All the nice girls, etc.

Written in 1909 by A. J. Mills (d. 1919)

186

Waiting at the Church

I'm in a nice bit of trouble, I confess;
Somebody with me has had a game.
I should by now be a proud and happy bride,
But I've still got to keep my single name.
I was proposed to by Obadiah Binks
In a very gentlemanly way;
Lent him all my money so that he could buy a home,
And punctually at twelve o'clock today –
   There was I, waiting at the church,
     Waiting at the church,
     Waiting at the church;
   When I found he'd left me in the lurch,
   Lor, how it did upset me!
   All at once, he sent me round a note –
     Here's the very note,
     This is what he wrote:
   'Can't get away to marry you today,
   My wife won't let me!'

Lor, what a fuss Obadiah made of me
When he used to take me in the park!
He used to squeeze me till I was black and blue,
When he kissed me he used to leave a mark.
Each time he met me he treated me to port,
Took me now and then to see the play;
Understand me rightly, when I say he treated me,
It wasn't *him* but *me* that used to pay.
   There was I, etc.

Just think how disappointed I must feel,
I'll be off me crumpet very soon.
I've lost my husband – the one I never had!
And I dreamed so about the honeymoon.
I'm looking out for another Obadiah,
I've already bought the wedding ring,
There's all my little fal-the-riddles packed up in my box –
Yes, absolutely two of ev'rything.
   There was I, etc.

Written by Fred W. Leigh (d. 1924)
Sung by Vesta Victoria

Any Old Iron?

Just a week or two ago my poor old Uncle Bill
Went and kicked the bucket and he left me in his will.
The other day I popped around to see poor Auntie Jane,
She said, 'Your Uncle Bill has left to you a watch and chain.'
I put it on right across my vest,
Thought I looked a dandy as it dangled on my chest.
Just to flash it off I started walking round about.
A lot of kiddies followed me and all began to shout:
    Any old iron, any old iron,
    Any any old, old iron?
    You look neat, talk about a treat,
    You look dapper from your napper to your feet.
    Dressed in style, brand new tile,
    And your father's old green tie on,
    But I wouldn't give you tuppence for your old watch chain,
    Old iron, old iron?

I went to the City once and thought I'd have a spree.
The Mayor of London, he was there, that's who I went to see.
He dashed up in a canter with a carriage and a pair.
I shouted 'Holler boys!' and threw my cap up in the air.
Just then the Mayor he began to smile,
Saw my face and then he shouted 'Lumme, what a dial!'
Started a-Lord Mayor-ing and I thought that I should die
When pointing to my watch and chain he hollered to me, Hi!
    Any old iron, etc.

Just to have a little bit of fun the other day,
Made up in my watch and chain I went and drew my pay,
Then got out with a lot of other Colonels 'on the loose',
I got full right up to here in fourp'nny 'stagger juice'.
One of them said 'We want a pot of ale.
Run him to the rag-shop and we'll bung him on the scale.'
I heard the fellow say, 'What's in this bundle that you've got?'
Then whisper to me kindly: 'Do you want to lose your lot?'
    Any old iron, etc.

Shan't forget when I got married to Selina Brown.
The way the people laughed at me it made me feel a clown.
I began to wonder, when their dials began to crack,
If by mistake I'd got my Sunday trousers front to back.
I wore my chain on my darby kell,
The sun was shining on it and it made me look a swell.
The organ started playing and the bells began to ring,
My chain began to rattle, so the choir began to sing.
    Any old iron, etc.

Written in 1910
by Charles Collins,
E. A. Shephard
and Fred Terry

Sung by Harry Champion

188

I'm Henery the Eighth, I am!

You don't know what you're looking at, now have a look at me!
I'm a bit of nob, I am – belong to Royaltee.
I'll tell you how it came about; I married Widow Burch,
And I was king of England when I toddled out of church.
Outside the people started shouting 'Hip-hooray!'
Said I, 'Get down upon your knees, it's Coronation Day!'
   I'm Henery the Eighth, I am !
   Henery the Eighth I am! I am!
   I got married to the widow next door,
   She'd been married seven times before.
   Every one was a Henery,
   She wouldn't have a Willie or a Sam.
   I'm her eighth old man named Henery,
   I'm Henery the Eighth I am.

I left the Duke of Cumberland, a pub up in the town,
Soon with one or two moochers I was holding up the Crown,
I sat upon the bucket that the carmen think they own;
Surrounded by my subjects, I was sitting on the throne.
Out came the pot-man saying, 'Go on home to bed!'
Said I, 'Now, say another word, and off'll go your head!'
   I'm Henery the Eighth, etc.

Now at the Waxwork Exhibition not so long ago
I was sitting among the kings, I made a lovely show.
To good old Queen Elizabeth I shouted, 'Wotcher Liz!'
While people poked my ribs and said, 'I wonder who this is?'
One said, 'It's Charlie Peace!' and then I got the spike.
I shouted, 'Show yer ignorance!' as waxy as you like.

The undertaker called and to the wife I heard him say,
'Have you got any orders, mum? We're rather slack today!
I packed up all your other seven for the golden gates;
Let's have a pound upon account for Henery the Eighth.'
But when he measured me with half a yard of string,
I dropped upon my marrow bones and sang 'God save the King!'
   I'm Henery the Eighth, etc.

Written and composed in 1910 by Fred Murray (d. 1922) and
R. P. Weston (d. 1936)

189

Daddy Wouldn't Buy me a Bow Wow

I love my little cat I do,
Its coat is oh so warm,
It comes each day with me to school
And sits upon the form.
When teacher says 'Why do you bring
That little pet of yours?'
I tell her that I bring my cat
Along with me because ...
    Daddy wouldn't buy me a bow wow,
    Daddy wouldn't buy me a bow wow.
    I've got a little cat,
    I am very fond of that,
    But I'd rather have a bow wow wow.

We used to have two tiny dogs,
Such pretty little dears,
But Daddy sold them 'cause they used
To bite each other's ears;
I cried all day. At eight at night
Papa sent me to bed.
When Ma came home and wiped my eyes,
I cried again and said ...
    Daddy wouldn't buy, etc.

I'll be so glad when I get old
To do just as I please.
I'll have a dozen bow wows then,
A parrot and some bees;
Whene'er I see a tiny pet
I'll kiss the litle thing,
'Twill remind me of the time gone by,
When I would cry, and sing ...
    Daddy wouldn't buy, etc.

Written and composed by Joseph Tabrar 1857–1931
Sung by Vesta Victoria

Who Were You With Last Night?

In an office up the West, Obadiah, smartly dressed,
Wandered in one Friday morn in a brand new fancy vest.
His pals all rose and said, 'My word, you're a naughty boy.
Last night we saw you making eyes at a nice little lump of joy,
You kissed her twice on the same place twice, and gave her waist a squeeze,
So we'd like you to inform us, Mister Obadiah, please,'
    Who were you with last night?
    Who were you with last night?
    It wasn't your sister, it wasn't your Ma,
    Ah! ah! ah! ah! ah! ah! ah! ah!
    Who were with you last night
    Out in the pale moonlight?
    Are you going to tell your Missus when you get home,
    Who were you with last night?

Like a rosy apple red, Obadiah blushed and said,
'You're mistaken, boys, because I was out with Uncle Fred.'
His pals looked round and winked, then said, as they gave a knowing grin,
Do you always squeeze your Uncle's waist, and tickle his bristly chin?
Does your Uncle too wear a high heeled shoe, and a dainty powdered face?
Does he sport a hobbled skirt and bits of furbelows and lace?'
    Who were you with, etc.

Obadiah said, 'I'm sure, my Brother, p'raps, you fellows saw.'
They said 'Wow-wow, Obadiah, you can tell that tale to Noah.
We knew you by your sprightly walk, and the tale you told was grand.
Last night we saw you in the park there listening to the band.
Your darling wife, she would have your life, and put your hair in curl,
If she knew you'd been out walking with some other little girl!'
    Who were you with, etc.

Fred Godfrey and Mark Sheridan, 1912

Hello! Hello! Who's your Lady Friend?

Jeremiah Jones, a lady's man was he.
Ev'ry pretty girl he loved to spoon;
Till he found a wife and down beside the sea
Went to Margate for the honeymoon.
But when he
Strolled along the promenade
With his little wife, just newly wed,
He got an awful scare when someone strolling there
Came up to him and winked and said,
   Hello! hello! who's your lady friend?
   Who's the little girlie by your side?
   I've seen you – with a girl or two –
   Oh! oh! oh! I *am* surprised at you.
   Hello! hello! stop your little games –
   Don't you think your ways ought to mend?
   It isn't the girl I saw you with at Brighton.
   Who – who – who's your lady friend?

Jeremiah took his wife's mamma one night
Round to see a moving picture show.
There upon the screen a picture came in sight.
Jeremiah cried, 'We'd better go,'
For on that
Picture there was Jeremiah
With a pretty girl upon his knee;
Ma cried, 'What does it mean?' then pointing to the screen,
The people yelled at Jones with glee,
   Hello! hello! etc.

Jeremiah now has settled down in life,
Said goodbye to frills and furbelows:
Never thinks of girls except his darling wife,
Always takes her everywhere he goes.
By Jove, why!
There he is – you naughty boy!
With a lady too – you're rather free.
Of course, you'll stake your life – the lady is your wife,
But tell me on the strict Q.T.,
   Hello! hello! etc.

Christmas pantomimes were Jones's chief delight,
Once he madly loved the Fairy Queen;
There behind the scenes, he spooned with her one night,
Someone for a lark pulled up the scenes.
And there was
Poor old Jones upon the stage
With his arm around the lady fair.
The house began to roar, from gall'ry down to floor,
Then ev'ry body shouted there,
    Hello! hello! etc.

Worton David and Bert Lee, 1913

The Cobbler's Song (Chu Chin Chow)

I sit and cobble at slippers and shoon
From the rise of sun to the set of moon:
Cobble and cobble as best I may,
Cobble all night and cobble all day,
And I sing as I cobble this doleful lay.

The stouter I cobble the less I earn,
For the soles ne'er crack nor the uppers turn,
The better my work, the less my pay,
But work can only be done one way.

And as I cobble with needle and thread
I judge the world by the way they tread:
Heels worn thick and heels worn thin,
Toes turned out and toes turned in,
There's food for thought in a sandal skin.

For prince and commoner, poor and rich,
Stand in need of the cobbler's stitch,
Why then worry what lies before,
Hangs this life by a thread, no more.

Written in 1916 by Oscar Asche 1871–1936
Composed by Frederick Norton

Don't Dilly-Dally on the Way

We had to move away,
'Cos the rent we couldn't pay,
The moving van came round just after dark;
There was me and my old man,
Shoving things inside the van,
Which we'd often done before, let me remark.
We packed all that could be packed
In the van and that's a fact;
And we got inside all we could get inside.
Then we packed all we could pack
On the tailboard at the back,
Till there wasn't any room for me to ride.
   My old man said, 'Follow the van,
   Don't dilly-dally on the way!'
   Off went the van with the home packed in it,
   I walked behind with my old cock linnet.
   But I dillied and dallied, dallied and dillied,
   Lost the van and don't know where to roam.
I stopped on the way to have the old half-quartern
And I can't find my way home.

I gave a helping hand
With the marble wash-hand-stand,
And straight, we wasn't getting on so bad;
All at once the car-man bloke
Had an accident and broke,
Well, the nicest bit of china that we had.
You'll understand of course,
I was cross about the loss,
Same as any other human woman would;
But I soon got over that,
What with 'two-out' and a chat,
'Cos it's little things like that what does you good.
   My old man, etc.
Now who's going to put up the old iron bedstead
If I can't find my way home?

Oh! I'm in such a mess –
I don't know the new address –
Don't even know the blessed neighbourhood,
And I feel as if I might
Have to stay out all the night,
And that ain't a-going to do me any good.
I don't make no complaint,
But I'm coming over faint,
What I want now is a good substantial feed,
And I sort o' kind o' feel,
If I don't soon have a meal,
I shall have to rob the linnet of his seed.
    My old man, etc.
You can't trust the 'specials' like the old time coppers
When you can't find your way home.

Written and composed in 1919 by Charles Collins (d. 1923)
and Fred W. Leigh (d. 1924)
Sung by Marie Lloyd

I Belong to Glasgow

I've been wi' a few o' ma cronies,
One or two pals o' ma ain.
We went in a hotel, where we did very well,
And then we came out once again.
Then we went into another,
And that is the reason I'm fou.
We had six deoch and dorises, then sang a chorus,
Just listen, I'll sing it to you.

    I belong to Glasgow, dear old Glasgow town!
    But there's something the matter wi' Glasgow
    For it's going round and round.
    I'm only a common old working chap,
    As anyone here can see,
    But when I get a couple of drinks on a Saturday,
    Glasgow belongs to me.

There's nothing in being teetotal,
And saving a shilling or two.
If your money you spend, you've nothing to lend,
Well, that's all the better for you.
There's nae harm in taking a drappie;
It ends all your trouble and strife:
It gives you a feeling, that when you get home
You don't care a hang for the wife.

    I belong to Glasgow, etc.

Written and sung by Will Fyffe 1885–1947

Leanin'

Sowin's pretty good,
Reapin' ain't so bad,
Scarin' of the crows suits a farmer's lad.
But if you axes me,
The thing that suits a feller
Is a little bit of straw to suck
To keep your fancies meller,
When you're
Leanin' on the gate beside the pond that lies beside the side of farmer's stacks
    of new mown hay,
It's just atwix the ricks beside the barn where farmer sticks inside the chicks
    he only hatched today;
Leanin', leanin',
I'm champion down our way, they say!
At leanin' on the gate beside the pond that lies beside the side of farmer's
    stacks of new mown hay,
That he's been gleanin' while I've been leanin'
All day.

Had a lurcher once,
Better than a gal;
Poacher? well a bit,
But he was a pal.
Now there's just a mound
Underneath the ellum,
Reckon folks would laff at oi
If I was to tell 'em
Why I'm
Leanin' on the gate beside the pond that lies beside the hedge where my old
    dog would play,
It's just acos from there I see the sunlight glintin' through the tree upon the
    grave where 'e do lie.
Sleepin', sleepin',
Goodbye is hard to say; that's why
I'm leanin' on the gate beside the pond that lies beside the side of farmer's
    stacks of new mown hay,
And at the gleanin'
He'll find me leanin'
All day.

Hugh E. Wright, 1926

197

Mad Dogs and Englishmen

In tropical climes there are certain times of day
When all the citizens retire
To tear their clothes off and perspire,
It's one of those rules that the greatest fools obey,
Because the sun is much too sultry
And one must avoid its ultry-violet ray.

Papalaka papalaka papalaka boo,
Papalaka papalaka papalaka boo,
Digariga digariga digariga doo,
Digariga digariga digariga doo!

The natives grieve when the white men leave their huts,
Because they're obviously, definitely nuts!

Mad dogs and Englishmen
Go out in the midday sun,
The Japanese don't care to,
The Chinese wouldn't dare to,
Hindoos and Argentines sleep firmly from twelve to one,
But Englishmen detest a siesta.
In the Phillipines
There are lovely screens
To protect you from the glare,
In the Malay States
There are hats like plates
Which the Britishers won't wear.
At twelve noon
The natives swoon
And no further work is done,
But mad dogs and Englishmen
Go out in the midday sun.

It's such a surprise for the Eastern eyes to see
That though the English are effete
They're quite impervious to heat,
When the white man rides every native hides in glee,
Because the simple creatures hope he
Will impale his solar topee on a tree.

Bolyboly bolyboly bolyboly baa,
Bolyboly bolyboly bolyboly baa,
Habaninny habaninny habaninny haa.
Habaninny habaninny habaninny haa.

It seems such a shame
When the English claim
The earth
That they give rise to such hilarity and mirth.

Mad dogs and Englishmen
Go out in the midday sun.
The toughest Burmese bandit
Can never understand it.
In Rangoon the heat of noon
Is just what the natives shun,
They put their Scotch or rye down
And lie down.

In a jungle town
Where the sun beats down
To the rage of man and beast
The English garb
Of the English sahib
Merely gets a bit more creased.
In Bangkok
At twelve o'clock
They foam at the mouth and run,
But mad dogs and Englishmen
Go out in the midday sun.

Mad dogs and Englishmen
Go out in the midday sun.
The smallest Malay rabbit
Deplores this stupid habit.
In Hongkong
They strike a gong
And fire off a noonday gun
To reprimand each inmate
Who's in late.

In the mangrove swamps
Where the python romps
There is peace from twelve to two,
Even caribous
Lie around and snooze
For there's nothing else to do.
In Bengal
To move at all
Is seldom, if ever, done,
But mad dogs and Englishmen
Go out in the midday sun.

Written and composed by Noël Coward (1899–1973)
Sung by Beatrice Lillie in 1931

Mrs Worthington, Don't Put your Daughter on the Stage

Regarding yours, dear Mrs Worthington,
Of Wednesday the 23rd,
Although your baby,
May be,
Keen on a stage career,
How can I make it clear,
That this is not a good idea.
For her to hope,
Dear Mrs Worthington,
Is on the face of it absurd,
Her personality
Is not in reality
Inviting enough,
Exciting enough
For this particular sphere.

Don't put your daughter on the stage, Mrs Worthington,
Don't put your daughter on the stage,
The profession is overcrowded
And the struggle's pretty tough
And admitting the fact
She's burning to act,
That isn't quite enough.
She has nice hands, to give the wretched girl her due,
But don't you think her bust is too
Developed for her age,
I repeat
Mrs Worthington,
Sweet
Mrs Worthington,
Don't put your daughter on the stage.

Don't put your daughter on the stage,
Mrs Worthington,
Don't put your daughter on the stage,
Though they said at the school of acting
She was lovely as Peer Gynt,
I'm afraid on the whole
An ingénue role
Would emphasise her squint.

She's a big girl, and though her teeth are fairly good
She's not the type I ever would
Be eager to engage,
No more buts,
Mrs Worthington,
NUTS,
Mrs Worthington,
Don't put your daughter on the stage.

Don't put your daughter on the stage, Mrs Worthington,
Don't put your daughter on the stage,
She's a bit of an ugly duckling
You must honestly confess,
And the width of her seat
Would surely defeat
Her chances of success,
It's a loud voice, and though it's not exactly flat,
She'll need a little more than that
To earn a living wage.
On my knees,
Mrs Worthington,
Please! Mrs Worthington.
Don't put your daughter on the stage.

Don't put your daughter on the stage, Mrs Worthington,
Don't put your daughter on the stage,
One look at her bandy legs should prove
She hasn't got a chance,
In addition to which
The son of a bitch
Can neither sing nor dance,
She's a *vile* girl and uglier than mortal sin,
One look at her has put me in
A tearing bloody rage,
That sufficed,
Mrs Worthington,
Christ!
Mrs Worthington,
Don't put your daughter on the stage.

Written and composed by Noël Coward. Sung by the author in 1935

Acknowledgements

The following songs are reproduced by permission of EMI Music Publishing Ltd, London WC2:

'Sussex by the Sea' W. Ward-Higgs © 1907 Darewski Music Pub. Ltd; 'Pack up your troubles' George Asaf © 1915 Francis Day & Hunter Ltd; 'Take me back to dear old Blighty' Mills Godfrey and Scott © 1916 B. Feldman & Co; 'Bless 'em all' Hughes and Lake © 1940 Keith Prowse Music; 'The White Cliffs of Dover' Nat Burton © 1941 Shapiro Bernstein & Co. Inc. (USA) sub-published by B. Feldman and Co. Ltd. (UK); 'There's a long long trail' Stoddard King © 1914 West's Ltd., London (UK); 'I'll be seeing you' Irving Kahl © 1938 Marlo Music Corp (USA) now Chappell & Co., Inc. (USA) sub-published by Francis Day & Hunter Ltd (UK); 'A Nightingale Sang in Berkeley Square' Manning Sherwin © 1940 Peter Maurice Music Co. Ltd., London (UK); 'Lilli Marlene' Hans Leip © 1944 Appolo Verlag (Germany) sub-published by Peter Maurice Co., Ltd, London (UK); 'Two lovely black eyes' Charles Coborn © 1886 Francis, Day & Hunter Ltd; 'She was one of the early birds' T. W. Connor © 1895 Francis, Day & Hunter Ltd; 'Down at the old Bull and Bush' Sterling, Hunting and Krone © 1903 Harry von Tilzer Music Pub. Co. USA; 'I'm Henery the Eighth I am' R. P. Weston and Fred Murray © 1910 Francis, Day & Hunter Ltd, London; 'The Cobbler's Song' Oscar Asche © 1916 Keith Prowse Music; 'I belong to Glasgow' Will Fyffe © 1921 Francis, Day & Hunter Ltd.

The following songs are reproduced by permission of Chappel Music Ltd; 'Because' Edward Teschemacher © 1911 Chappell and Co. Ltd; 'I'll walk beside you' Edward Lockton © 1936 Chappell Music Ltd; 'Waltzing Matilda' A. B. Pateson © 1940 Allan & Co. Pty. Ltd. Reproduced by permission of Ascherberg, Hopwood and Crew Ltd. 'Mad dogs and Englishmen' and 'Mrs Worthington' Noël Coward © 1935 Chappell Music Ltd. are used by permission of the Noël Coward Estate.

'If you were the only girl in the world' Clifford Grey is used by permission of Redwood Music Ltd.

Permission to use copyright material is also gratefully acknowledged to the following: Peter Newbolt for 'Drake's Drum' by Sir Henry Newbolt; The Society of Authors as the literary representative of the Estate of John Masefield for 'Sea-Fever'; The Society of Authors as the literary representative of the Estate of A. E. Housman, and Jonathan Cape Ltd, for 'Bredon Hill'; A. P. Watt Ltd as the literary representative of the Rudyard Kipling Estate for 'Recessional', 'Boots' and 'The Road to Mandalay'.

Index of First Lines

Index of Authors